Applied Project Management

Applied CQRM Book Series

Volume VI

Applying Monte Carlo Risk Simulation, Strategic Real Options, Stochastic Forecasting, Portfolio Optimization, and Data and Decision Analytics

IIPER Press

IIPER
Press

Johnathan Mun, Ph.D.

California, USA

RQV Project Economics Analysis Tool

For Jayden, Emma, and Penny.

In a world where risk and uncertainty abound, you are the only constants in my life.

Dedicated in loving memory of my mom.

Delight yourself in the Lord and He will give you the desires of your heart.

Psalm 37:4

The Applied CQRM Book Series showcases how the advanced analytics covered in the Certified in Quantitative Risk Management (CQRM) certification program can be applied to real-life business problems. In Volume VI, we show how to model and risk simulate complex projects to obtain schedule and cost risks.

Pragmatic applications are emphasized in order to demystify the many elements inherent in risk analysis. A black box will remain a black box if no one can understand the concepts despite its power and applicability. It is only when the black box methods become transparent, so that researchers can understand, apply, and convince others of their results, value-add, and applicability, that the approaches will receive widespread attention. This transparency is achieved through step-by-step applications of quantitative modeling as well as through presenting multiple cases and discussing real-life applications.

This book is targeted at those individuals who have completed the CQRM certification program but can also be used by anyone familiar with basic quantitative research methods—there is something for everyone. It is also applicable for use as a second-year MBA/MS-level or introductory PhD textbook. The examples in the book assume some prior knowledge of the subject matter.

Additional information on the CQRM program can be obtained at:

www.iiper.org

www.realoptionsvaluation.com

www.rovusa.com

Dr. Johnathan C. Mun is the founder, chairman, and CEO of Real Options Valuation, Inc. (ROV), a consulting, training, and software development firm specializing in strategic real options, financial valuation, Monte Carlo risk simulation, stochastic forecasting, optimization, decision analytics, business intelligence, healthcare analytics, enterprise risk management, project risk management, quantitative research methods, and risk analysis located in northern Silicon Valley, California. ROV has partners around the world including Argentina, Beijing, Chicago, China, Colombia, Ghana, Hong Kong, India, Italy, Japan, Malaysia, Mexico City, New York, Nigeria, Peru, Puerto Rico, Russia, Saudi Arabia, Shanghai, Singapore, Slovenia, South Africa, South Korea, Spain, United Kingdom, Venezuela, Zurich, and others. ROV also has a local office in Shanghai.

Dr. Mun is also the chairman of the International Institute of Professional Education and Research (IIPER), an accredited global organization staffed by professors from named universities from around the world that provides the Certified in Quantitative Risk Management (CQRM) and Certified in Risk Management (CRM) designations, among others. He is the creator of many powerful software tools including Risk Simulator, Real Options SLS Super Lattice Solver, Modeling Toolkit, Project Economics Analysis Tool (PEAT), Credit Market Operational Liquidity Risk (CMOL), Employee Stock Options Valuation, ROV BizStats, ROV Modeler Suite (Basel Credit Modeler, Risk Modeler, Optimizer, and Valuator), ROV Compiler, ROV Extractor and Evaluator, ROV Dashboard, ROV Quantitative Data Miner, and other software applications, as well as the ROV risk-analysis training DVD. He holds public seminars on risk analysis and CQRM programs. He has over 21 registered patents and patents pending globally. He has authored over 23 books published by John Wiley & Sons, Elsevier Science, IIPER Press, and ROV Press, including multiple volumes of the Applied CQRM Series (IIPER Press, 2019–2020); *Modeling Risk: Applying Monte Carlo Simulation, Strategic Real Options, Stochastic Forecasting, Portfolio Optimization, Data Analytics, Business Intelligence, and Decision Modeling,* First Edition (Wiley, 2006), Second Edition (Wiley, 2010), and Third Edition

(ROV Press, 2015); *The Banker's Handbook on Credit Risk* (2008); *Advanced Analytical Models: 250 Applications from Basel II Accord to Wall Street and Beyond* (2008); *Real Options Analysis: Tools and Techniques,* First Edition (2003), Second Edition (2005), and Third Edition (2016); *Real Options Analysis Course: Business Cases* (2003); *Applied Risk Analysis: Moving Beyond Uncertainty* (2003); and *Valuing Employee Stock Options* (2004). His books and software are being used at over 350 top universities around the world, including the Bern Institute in Germany, Chung-Ang University in South Korea, Georgetown University, ITESM in Mexico, Massachusetts Institute of Technology, U.S. Naval Postgraduate School, New York University, Stockholm University in Sweden, University of the Andes in Chile, University of Chile, University of Hull, University of Pennsylvania Wharton School, University of York in the United Kingdom, and Edinburgh University in Scotland, among others.

Currently a risk, finance, and economics professor, Dr. Mun has taught courses in financial management, investments, real options, economics, and statistics at the undergraduate and the graduate MS, MBA, and PhD levels. He teaches and has taught at universities all over the world, from the U.S. Naval Postgraduate School (Monterey, California) and University of Applied Sciences (Switzerland and Germany) as full professor, to Golden Gate University (California) and St. Mary's College (California), and has chaired many graduate research MBA thesis and PhD dissertation committees. He also teaches weeklong Risk Analysis, Real Options Analysis, and Risk Analysis for Managers public courses where participants can obtain the CRM and CQRM designations on completion. He is a senior fellow at the Magellan Center and sits on the board of standards at the American Academy of Financial Management.

He was formerly the Vice President of Analytics at Decisioneering, Inc., where he headed the development of options and financial analytics software products, analytical consulting, training, and technical support, and where he was the creator of the Real Options Analysis Toolkit software, the older and much less powerful predecessor of the Real Options Super Lattice software. Prior to joining Decisioneering, he was a Consulting Manager and Financial Economist in the Valuation Services and Global Financial Services practice of KPMG Consulting and a Manager with the Economic Consulting Services practice at KPMG LLP.

He has extensive experience in econometric modeling, financial analysis, real options, economic analysis, and statistics. During his tenure at Real Options Valuation, Inc., Decisioneering, and KPMG Consulting, he taught and consulted on a variety of real options, risk analysis, financial forecasting, project management, and financial valuation issues for more than 100 multinational firms (current and former clients include 3M, Airbus, Boeing, BP, Chevron Texaco, Financial Accounting Standards Board, Fujitsu, GE, Goodyear, Microsoft, Motorola, Northrop Grumman, Pfizer, Timken, U.S. Department of Defense, U.S. Navy, Veritas, and many others). His experience prior to joining KPMG included being department head of financial planning and analysis at Viking Inc. of FedEx, performing financial forecasting, economic analysis, and market research. Prior to that, he did financial planning and freelance financial consulting work.

Dr. Mun received a PhD in finance and economics from Lehigh University, where his research and academic interests were in the areas of investment finance, econometric modeling, financial options, corporate finance, and microeconomic theory. He also has an MBA in business administration, an MS in management science, and a BS in biology and physics. He is Certified in Financial Risk Management, Certified in Financial Consulting, and Certified in Quantitative Risk Management. He is a member of the American Mensa, Phi Beta Kappa Honor Society, and Golden Key Honor Society as well as several other professional organizations, including the Eastern and Southern Finance Associations, American Economic Association, and Global Association of Risk Professionals.

In addition, he has written many academic articles published in the *Journal of Expert Systems with Applications; Defense Acquisition Research Journal; American Institute of Physics Proceedings; Acquisitions Research (U.S. Department of Defense); Journal of the Advances in Quantitative Accounting and Finance; Global Finance Journal; International Financial Review; Journal of Financial Analysis; Journal of Applied Financial Economics; Journal of International Financial Markets, Institutions and Money; Financial Engineering News;* and *Journal of the Society of Petroleum Engineers.* Finally, he has contributed chapters in dozens of books and written over a hundred technical whitepapers, newsletters, case studies, and research papers for Real Options Valuation, Inc.

JohnathanMun@cs.com

San Francisco, California

ACCOLADES FOR DR. MUN'S BOOKS

...powerful toolset for portfolio/program managers to make rational choices among alternatives...
>
> Rear Admiral James Greene (Ret.), Acquisitions Chair
> Naval Postgraduate School (USA)

...unavoidable for any professional...logical, concrete, and conclusive approach...
>
> Jean Louis Vaysse, Vice President, Airbus (France)

...proven, revolutionary approach to quantifying risks and opportunities in an uncertain world...
>
> Mike Twyman, President, Mission Solutions,
> Cubic Global Defense, Inc. (USA)

...must read for anyone running investment economics...best way to quantify risk and strategic options...
>
> Mubarak A. Alkhater, Executive Director, New Business,
> Saudi Electric Co. (Saudi Arabia)

... pragmatic powerful risk techniques, valuable theoretical insights and analytics useful in any industry...
>
> Dr. Robert S. Finocchiaro, Director,
> Corporate R&D Services, 3M (USA)

...most important risk tools in one volume, definitive source on risk management with vivid examples...
>
> Dr. Ricardo Valerdi, Engineering Systems,
> Massachusetts Institute of Technology (USA)

...step-by-step complex concepts with unmatched ease and clarity... a "must read" for all professionals...
>
> Dr. Hans Weber, Product Development Leader,
> Syngenta AG (Switzerland)

...clear step-by-step approach...latest technology in decision making for real-world business...
>
> Dr. Paul W. Finnegan, Vice President,
> Alexion Pharmaceuticals (USA)

...clear roadmap and breadth of topics to create dynamic risk-adjusted strategies and options...
>
> Jeffrey A. Clark, Vice President Strategic Planning,
> The Timken Company (USA)

…clearly organized and tool-supported exploration of real-life business risks, options, strategy…
>   Robert Mack, Vice President, Distinguished Analyst,
>   Gartner Group (USA)

…full range of methodologies for quantifying and mitigating risk for effective enterprise management…
>   Raymond Heika, Director of Strategic Planning,
>   Northrop Grumman Corporation (USA)

…a must-read for product portfolio managers…captures risk exposure of strategic investments…
>   Rafael Gutierrez, Executive Director Strategic Marketing Planning,
>   Seagate Technologies (USA)

…complex topics exceptionally explained…
can understand and practice…
>   Agustín Velázquez, Senior Economist,
>   Venezuela Central Bank (Venezuela)

…constant source of practical applications with risk management theory…simply excellent!
>   Alfredo Roisenzvit, Executive Director/Professor,
>   Risk-Business Latin America (Argentina)

…the best risk modeling book is now better…
required reading by all executives…
>   David Mercier, Vice President Corporate Dev.,
>   Bonanza Creek Energy [Oil & Gas] (USA)

…bridge of theory and practice, intuitive, understandable interpretations…
>   Luis Melo, Senior Econometrician,
>   Colombia Central Bank (Colombia)

…valuable tools for corporations to deliver value to shareholders and society even in rough times…
>   Dr. Markus Götz Junginger, Lead Partner,
>   Gallup (Germany)

CONTENTS

ANALYTICAL PROJECT MANAGEMENT IN A NUTSHELL

All organizations depend heavily on project planning tools to forecast when various projects will complete. Completing projects within specified times and budgets is critical to facilitate smooth business operations. In our high-technology environment, many things can impact schedule. Technical capabilities can often fall short of expectations. Requirements are insufficient in many cases and need further definition. Tests can bring surprising results—good or bad. A whole host of other reasons can lead to schedule slips. On rare occasions, we may run into good fortune and the schedule can be accelerated.

Project schedules are inherently uncertain, and change is normal. Therefore, we should expect changes and find the best way to deal with them. So why do projects always take longer than anticipated? One reason is inaccurate schedule estimating. The following discussion presents a description on shortcomings in the traditional methods of schedule estimation and how simulation and advanced analytics can be applied to address these shortcomings.

Traditional schedule management typically starts with a list of tasks. Next these tasks are put in order and linked from the predecessor to successor for each task. They are typically displayed in either a Gantt chart form or a network. For our discussion in this chapter, we concentrate on the network diagram. The duration for each task within the network is then developed. The estimated duration for each task is given a single-point estimate, even though we know from experience that this estimate should be a range of values. Therefore, the first mistake is using a single-point estimate. In addition, many people who provide duration estimates try to put their best foot forward and give an optimistic or best-case estimate. If we assume that the probability of achieving this best-case estimate for one task is 20%, then the likelihood of achieving the best case for two tasks is merely 4% (20% of 20%), and three tasks yields only 0.8%. Within a real project with many more tasks, there is only an infinitesimal chance of making the best-case schedule.

Once the task duration estimates have been developed, the network is constructed and the various paths through the network are traced. The task durations are summed along each of these paths, and the one that takes the longest is identified as the critical path.

Figure 1.1 illustrates an example network and critical path. The sum of task durations along the critical path is listed as the project completion date. In Figure 1.1, there are four paths through the network from beginning to end. The shortest/quickest path is Tasks 1-2-3-10-11 with a total duration of 22 days. The next shortest path is tasks 1-7-8-9-10-11 at 34 days, and then path 1-4-5-6-10-11 at 36 days. Finally, the path 1-4-8-9-10-11 takes the longest at 37 days and is the critical path for this network.

So let us assume that this network of tasks is our part of a larger effort and some other effort upstream of ours has overrun by a day. Our boss has asked us to shorten our schedule by one or two days to get the overall effort back on track. Traditional schedule management has one target: shorten the longest duration item in the critical path. Another approach is to shorten every task on the entire critical path. Because the first technique is more focused, more prone to success, and creates fewer conflicts on our team, let us assume that we will use that one. Hence, we will want to reduce Task 8 from 10 days to 9 days to shorten our schedule and we will satisfy our boss or our customer. Let us leave the traditional methodology at this stage feeling satisfied with our efforts, but curious about exploring alternatives. The next step is to explore simulation and risk analytics to enhance the management of the project. Specifically, we will be employing Monte Carlo risk simulations on each of the task's projected budget and schedule, resulting in a probabilistic and risk profile view of the entire network's cost and schedule.

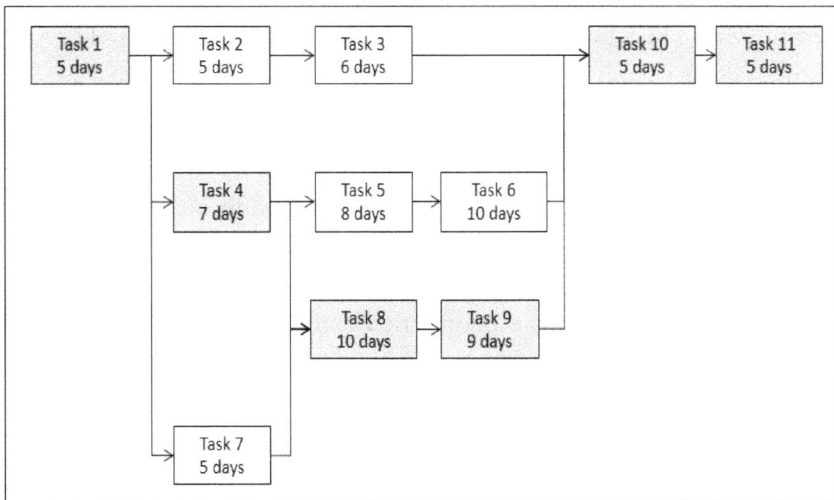

Figure 1.1: Network Schedule

If we agree that task durations can vary, then that uncertainty should be taken into account in schedule models. A schedule model can be developed by creating a probability distribution for each task, representing the likelihood of completing the particular task at a specific duration. Monte Carlo simulation techniques can then be applied to forecast the entire range of possible project durations.

A simple triangular distribution is a reasonable probability distribution to use to describe the uncertainty for a task's duration. It is a natural fit because if we ask someone to give a range of duration values for a specific task, he or she usually supplies two of the distribution's elements: the minimum duration and the maximum duration. We need only ask or determine the most likely duration to complete the triangular distribution. The parameters are simple, intuitively easy to understand, and readily accepted by customers and bosses alike. Other more complex distributions could be used such as the Beta or Weibull but little, if anything, is gained because the determination of the estimated parameters for these distributions is prone to error and the method of determination is not easily explainable to the customer or boss.

To get the best estimates, we should use multiple sources to get the estimates of the minimum, most likely, and maximum values for the task durations. We can talk to the contractor, the project manager, and the people doing the hands-on work and then compile a list of duration estimates. Historical data can also be used, but with caution because many efforts may be similar to past projects but usually contain several unique elements or combinations. We can use Figure 1.2 as a guide. Minimum values should reflect optimal utilization of resources. Maximum values should take into account substantial problems, but it is not necessary to account for the absolute worst case where everything goes wrong and the problems compound each other. Note that the most likely value will be the value experienced most often, but it is typically less than the median or mean in most cases. For our example problem, shown in Figure 1.1, the minimum, most likely, and maximum values given in Figure 1.3 will be used. We can use Risk Simulator's input assumptions to create triangular distributions based on these minimum, most likely, and maximum parameters. The column of dynamic duration values shown in Figure 1.3 was created by taking one random sample from each of the associated triangular distributions.

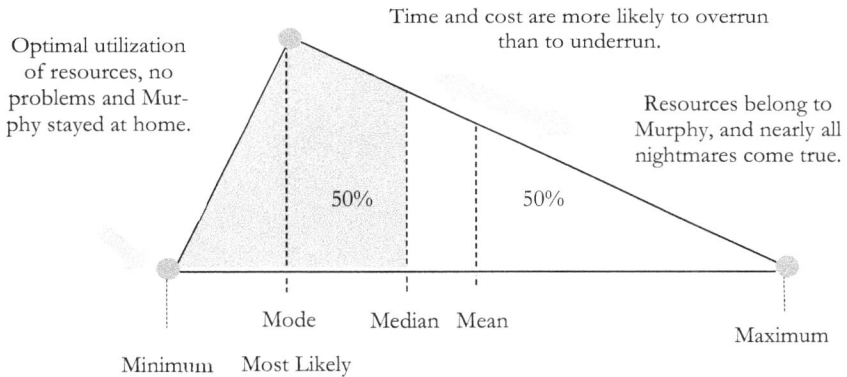

Figure 1.2: Triangular Distribution

After the triangular distributions are created, the next step is to use the schedule network to determine the paths. For the example problem shown Figure 1.1, there are four paths through the network from beginning to end. These paths are shown in Figure 1.4 with their associated durations. (Note: When setting up the spreadsheet for the various paths, it is absolutely essential to use the input assumptions for the task durations and then reference these task duration cells when calculating the duration for each path. This method ensures that the duration of individual tasks is the same regardless of which path is used.) The overall schedule total duration is the maximum of the four paths. In Risk

Simulator, we would designate that cell as an Output Forecast. In probabilistic schedule analysis, we are not concerned with the critical path/near-critical path situations because the analysis automatically accounts for all path durations through the calculations.

Task #	Task Name	Min	Likely	Max	Point Estimate
1	Stakeholder Analysis	4.5	5	6	5
2	Objectives Hierarchy	4.5	5	6	5
3	Decision Metrics Development	5.5	6	7	6
4	Functional Analysis	6	7	9	7
5	Primary Module Requirements	7	8	10	8
6	Primary Module Development	9	10	13	10
7	Secondary Module Functional Analysis	4.5	5	6	5
8	Secondary Module Requirements	9	10	12	10
9	Secondary Module Development	8	9	10	9
10	Trade Studies	2.5	3	4	3
11	Final Development Specification	2.5	3	4	3

Figure 1.3: Range of Task Durations

We can now use Risk Simulator and run a Monte Carlo simulation to produce a forecast for schedule duration. Figure 1.5 shows the results for the example problem. Let us return to the numbers given by the traditional method. The original estimate stated the project would be complete in 37 days. If we use the left-tail function on the forecast chart, we can determine the likelihood of completing the task in 37 days based on the Monte Carlo simulation. In this case, there is a mere 8.27% chance of completion within the 37 days. This result illustrates the second shortcoming in the traditional method: Not only is the point estimate incorrect, but it puts us in a high-risk overrun situation before the work has even started! As shown in Figure 1.5, the median value is 38.5 days. Some industry standards recommend using the 80% certainty value for most cases, which equates to 39.5 days in the example problem.

Path 1	Time 1	Path 2	Time 2	Path 3	Time 3	Path 4	Time 4
1	5.78	1	5.78	1	5.78	1	5.78
2	4.79	4	7.78	4	7.78	7	5.20
3	6.16	5	9.22	8	10.05	8	10.05
10	3.33	6	10.12	9	9.40	9	9.40
11	3.76	10	3.33	10	3.33	10	3.33
		11	3.76	11	3.76	11	3.76
Totals	23.82		39.99		40.10		37.52
Overall Total Schedule			40.10	(Max of all the totals)			

Figure 1.4: Paths and Durations for Example Problem

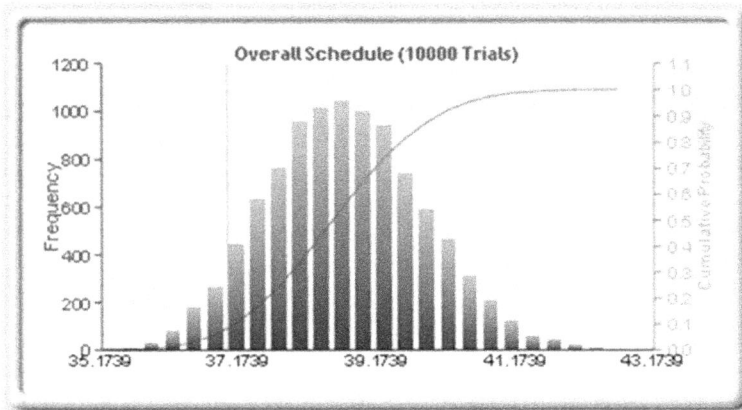

Type: Left-Tail ≤, Lower: -Infinity, Upper: 37.0000, Certainty: 8.2700%

Figure 1.5: Simulation Results

Now let us revisit the boss's request to reduce the whole schedule by one day. Where do we put the effort to reduce the overall duration? If we are using probabilistic schedule management, we do not use the critical path; so, where do we start? Using Risk Simulator's Tornado Analysis and Sensitivity Analysis tools, we can identify the most effective targets for reduction efforts. The tornado chart (Figure 1.6) identifies the most influential variables (tasks) to the overall schedule. This chart provides the best targets to reduce the mean/median values.

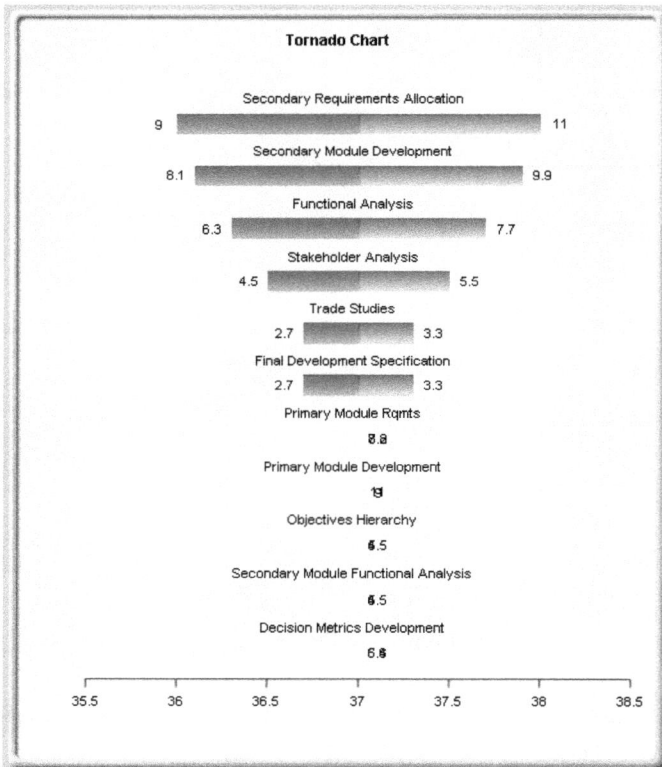

Figure 1.6: Tornado Analysis

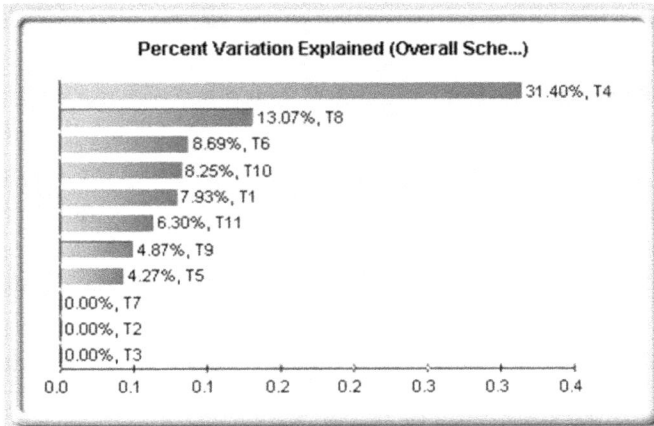

Percent Variation Explained (Overall Sche...)

- 31.40%, T4
- 13.07%, T8
- 8.69%, T6
- 8.25%, T10
- 7.93%, T1
- 6.30%, T11
- 4.87%, T9
- 4.27%, T5
- 0.00%, T7
- 0.00%, T2
- 0.00%, T3

| 0.0 | 0.1 | 0.1 | 0.2 | 0.2 | 0.3 | 0.3 | 0.4 |

Figure 1.7: Sensitivity Analysis

We cannot address the mean/median without addressing the variation, however. The Sensitivity Analysis tool shows what variables (tasks) contribute the most to the variation in the overall schedule output (see Figure 1.7). In this case, we can see that the variation in Task 4 is the major contributor to the variation in the overall schedule. Another interesting observation is that the variation in Task 6, a task not on the critical path, is also contributing nearly 9% of the overall variation.

In this example, reducing the schedule duration for Task 4, Task 8, and Task 9 would pay the most dividends as far as reducing the overall schedule length. Determining the underlying reasons for the substantial variation in Tasks 4, 6, and 8 would likely give better insight into these processes. For example, the variation in Task 4 may be caused by the lack of available personnel. Management actions could be taken to dedicate personnel to the effort and reduce the variation substantially, which would reduce the overall variation and enhance the predictability of the schedule. Digging into the reasons for variation will lead to targets where management actions will be most effective, much more so than by simply telling the troops to reduce their task completion time.

Using the network schedule model, we can also experiment to see how different reduction strategies may pay off. For example, taking one day out of Tasks 4, 8, and 9 under the traditional method would lead us to believe that a three-day reduction has taken place, but if we reduce the Most Likely value for Tasks 4, 8, and 9 by one day and run the Monte Carlo risk simulation, we find that the median value is still 37.91, or only a 0.7-day reduction. This small reduction proves that the variation must be addressed. If we reduce the variation by 50%, keeping the original minimum and the most likely values, but reducing the maximum value for each distribution, then we reduce the median from 38.5 to 37.91—about the same as reducing the most likely values. Taking both actions (reducing the most likely and maximum values) reduces the median to 36.83, giving us a 55% chance of completing within 37 days. This analysis proves that reducing the most likely value and the overall variation is the most effective action.

To get to 36 days, we need to continue to work down the list of tasks shown in the sensitivity and tornado charts addressing each task. If we give Task 1 the same treatment, reducing its most likely and maximum values, then completion within 36 days can be accomplished with a 51% certainty, and a 79.25% certainty of completing within 37 days. The maximum value for the overall schedule is reduced from more than 42 days to less than 40 days. Substantial management efforts would be needed, however, to reach 36 days at the 80% certainty level.

When managing the production schedule, use the best-case numbers. If we use the most likely values or, worse yet, the maximum values, production personnel will not strive to hit the best-case numbers thus implementing a self-fulfilling prophecy of delayed completion. When budgeting, we should create the budget for the median outcome but recognize that there is uncertainty in the real world as well as risk. When relating the schedule to the customer, provide the values that equate to the 75% to 80% certainty level. In most cases, customers prefer predictability (on-time completion) over potentially speedy completion that includes significant risk. Lastly, acknowledge that the "worst case" can conceivably occur and create contingency plans to protect your organization in case it does occur. If the "worst case"/maximum value is unacceptable, then make the appropriate changes in the process to reduce the maximum value of the outcome to an acceptable level.

Conclusion

With traditional schedule management, there is only one answer for the scheduled completion date. Each task gets one duration estimate and that estimate is accurate only if everything goes according to plan, which is not a likely occurrence. With probabilistic schedule management, thousands of trials are run exploring the range of possible outcomes for schedule duration. Each task in the network receives a time estimate distribution, accurately reflecting each task's uncertainty. Correlations can be entered to more accurately model real-world behavior. Critical paths and near-critical paths are automatically taken into account, and the output forecast distribution will accurately reflect the entire range of possible outcomes. Using tornado and sensitivity analyses, we can maximize the effectiveness of our management actions to control schedule variations and, if necessary, reduce the overall schedule at high certainty levels.

HANDS-ON PROJECT MANAGEMENT IN PEAT

As discussed in the previous chapter, within the world of project management, there are essentially two major sources of risks: schedule risk and cost risk. In other words, will the project be on time and under budget, or will there be a schedule crash and budget overrun, and, if so, how bad can they be? To illustrate how quantitative risk management can be applied to project management, we use ROV PEAT to model these two sources of risks. The following examples and illustrations assume that the reader has the PEAT software installed (the installation instructions are provided at the end of this book).

Simple Sequential Project Tasks

To follow along, start the PEAT software, select the *Project Management—Cost and Schedule Risk* module (Figure 2.1), and click on *Load Example*. The software will load with some example projects. We begin by illustrating a simple linear path project in the *Project D* tab (Figure 2.2). Click on this tab to get started. Note that users can click on the *Projects* menu to add additional projects or delete and rename existing projects. The example loaded has 5 sample predefined projects. In this simple linear path project (Project D), there are 11 sample tasks and each task would be linked to its subsequent tasks linearly (i.e., Task 2 can only start after Task 1 is done, and so forth). In each project tab, the user has a set of controls and inputs:

- *Sequential Path* versus *Complex Network Path*. The first example illustrated uses the sequential path, which means there is a simple linear progression of tasks. In the next example, we will explore the complex network path where tasks can be executed linearly and simultaneously, and can be recombined at any point in time.

- *Fixed Costs*. The fixed costs and their ranges suitable for risk simulation (minimum, most likely, maximum) are required inputs. These fixed costs are costs that will be incurred regardless of whether there is an overrun in schedule (the project can be completed early or late, but the fixed costs will be the same regardless).

- *Time Schedule*. This control is for setting the specific period time schedule (minimum, most likely, maximum) in days, weeks, or months. Users will first select the periodicity (e.g., days, weeks, months, or unitless) from the droplist and enter the projected time schedule per task. This schedule will be used in conjunction with the variable cost elements (see next bullet item) and will only be available if *Include Schedule-Based Cost Analysis* is checked.

- *Variable Cost*. This is the variable cost that is incurred based on the time schedule for each task. This variable cost is per period and will be multiplied by the number of periods to obtain the total variable cost for each task. The sum of all fixed costs and variable costs for all tasks will, of course, be the total cost for the project (denoted as *Project Total Cost*).

- *Overrun Assumption*. This is a percent budget buffer or cushion to include in each task. This column is only available and used if *Include Budget Overruns and Buffers* checkbox is selected. See Chapter 6 for more details on this functionality and associated calculations.

- *Probability of Success.* This allows users to enter the probability of each task being successful. If a task fails, then all subsequent tasks will be canceled, and the costs will not be incurred, as the project stops and is abandoned. This column is available and will be used in the risk simulation only if *Include Probabilities of Success* checkbox is selected. See Chapter 6 for more details on this functionality.

- *Run* and *Run All Projects.* These run buttons will perform the relevant computations based on the settings and inputs, and also run risk simulations if the *Perform Risk Simulation* checkbox is selected (as well as if the requisite simulation settings such as distribution type, number of trials, and seed value settings are entered appropriately). This will run the current project's model. If multiple projects need to be run, you can click on the *Run All Projects* button instead. By default, all projects are run simultaneously. If the checkbox *Run Sequentially* is selected, the simulation will be run on one project at a time.

Real Options Valuation

Project Economics Analysis Tool

© Copyright 2012-2018 Real Options Valuation. Inc.

○ Corporate Investments - Stochastic DCF
○ Enterprise Risk Management (ERM) - Risk Register
◉ Project Management - Schedule and Cost Risk
○ Goals Analytics - Sales and Pipeline Modeling
○ Banking - Credit, Market, Operational, Liquidity Risk
○ Corporate Investments - Buy vs. Lease
○ Public Sector Analysis - Knowledge Value Added
○ Oil and Gas Economics - Investment Decision Analysis
○ Oil and Gas Economics - Oil Field Reserves
○ Oil and Gas Economics - Remaining Oil Recovery
○ Oil and Gas Economics - Well Type Curves
○ Customized Encrypted Models

Applying Integrated Risk Management methodologies (Monte Carlo risk simulation, strategic real options, stochastic forecasting, business analytics, and portfolio optimization) to project and portfolio economics and financial analysis.

| Load Example | English | ⌄ |

| Start Selected Module | Exit |

☐ Healthcare - Health Economics Analysis Tool (HEAT) ⌄

Figure 2.1: PEAT—Project Management Module

To see which of the input assumptions drive total cost and schedule the most, a tornado analysis can be executed (Figure 2.3). Tornado analysis is a powerful analytical technique that captures the static impacts of each variable on the outcome of the model; that is, the tool automatically perturbs each variable in the model a preset amount, captures the fluctuation on the model's forecast or final result, and lists the resulting perturbations ranked from the most significant to the least. Figure 2.3 illustrates the application of a tornado analysis, where Project D's Expected Project Cost is selected as the target result to be analyzed. The target result's precedents in the model are used in creating the tornado chart. Precedents are all the input and intermediate variables that affect the outcome of the model. For instance, if the model consists of $A = B + C$, and where $C = D + E$, then B, D, and E, are the precedents for A (C is not a precedent as it is only an intermediate calculated value). Figure 2.3 also shows the testing range of each precedent variable used to estimate the target result. If the precedent variables are simple inputs, then the testing range will be a simple perturbation based on the range chosen (e.g., the default is $\pm 10\%$). Each precedent variable can be perturbed at different percentages if required (see the data grid at the bottom of the user interface). A wider range is important as it is better able to test extreme values rather than smaller perturbations around the expected values. In certain circumstances, extreme values may have a larger, smaller, or unbalanced impact (e.g., nonlinearities may occur where increasing or decreasing economies of scale and scope creep in for larger or smaller values of a variable) and only a wider range will capture this nonlinear impact.

The model can then be Monte Carlo risk simulated based on the minimum, most likely, and maximum values that were entered previously (Figure 2.2) and the results will show probability distributions of cost and schedule (Figure 2.4). For instance, the sample results show that for Project D, there is a 95% probability that the project can be completed at a cost of $398,742. The expected median or most likely value was originally $377,408 (Figure 2.2). With simulation, it shows that to be 95% sure that there are sufficient funds to complete the project, an additional buffer of $21,334 is warranted.

Note that the simulation chart in Figure 2.4 shows a trimodal distribution, i.e., there are three clusters and peaks in the histogram. This is because a probability of success on each task is set up in the model. See Chapter 6 for more details on how the overrun and probability of success works in the computations. Also refer to the appendices for more details on interpreting the distributional moments, simulation statistics, and the shape and characteristics of distributions.[1]

---

[1]The results illustrated were obtained using the default example's 1,000 simulation trials with a seed value of 123 for all Projects A through D, and simulations were set to run all projects simultaneously. In real-life projects, we recommend running 1,000–10,000 simulation trials depending on the complexity of the model.

File   Edit   Projects   Report   Tools   Language   Decimals   Help

Welcome to the ROV Project Economics Analysis Tool (PEAT). This module will help you model your Project Management's Dynamic Risk-Based Schedule and Cost Analysis. It enables you to build your own Complex Task-Based Project Network, model and identify the Critical Path, and apply Monte Carlo Risk Simulation and Sensitivity Analysis to determine the cost and schedule uncertainties.

Project Management   Applied Analytics   Risk Simulation   Options Strategies   Options Valuation   Forecast Prediction   Dashboard   Knowledge Center

Project A   Project B   Project C   Project D   Project E   Portfolio Analysis

Select the Project Schedule & Cost Risk Model to use: ● Sequential Path   ○ Complex Network Path   Project Name/Notes:

Schedule & Cost
☑ Include Schedule-Based Cost Analysis   ☑ Perform Risk Simulation
☑ Include Budget Overrun & Buffers   ☑ Apply Seed Value: 1,000
☑ Include Probabilities of Success of Each Task and Model Their Impacts

Simulation Trials: 123
Tasks with   Weekly   Show   11

Run   Run All Projects
☑ Auto Update   ☐ Run Sequentially
Triangular

Task	Task Name	Cost (Fixed Cost)			Computed Cost	Time Schedule (Weeks)			Variable Weekly Cost	Overrun Assumption	Probability of Success	Linked Events
		Minimum	Most Likely	Maximum		Minimum	Most Likely	Maximum				
Task 1	Conceptualization	1,500	2,250	4,500	5,585	1.6	2.15	3.8	1,500	2.00%	95.00%	1
Task 2	Added time for remodeling product	150	750	1,500	2,325	0.61	1.05	1.6	1,500	0.00%	95.00%	1
Task 3	Initiation	5,000	7,500	12,500	18,700	2.7	3.8	6	2,500	10.00%	93.00%	1
Task 4	Reworking concept	750	1,500	3,000	3,900	1.05	1.6	2.7	1,500	0.00%	99.00%	1
Task 5	Modification of existing concepts	750	1,500	2,250	3,900	1.05	1.6	2.15	1,500	0.00%	99.00%	1
Task 6	Phase 2 Development	17,500	21,000	28,000	52,572	6	7.1	9.3	3,500	15.00%	97.00%	1
Task 7	Additional R&D	1,000	1,500	2,000	3,723	1.6	2.15	2.7	1,000	2.00%	97.00%	1
Task 8	Apply external IP	2,500	5,000	5,000	13,260	1.05	1.6	1.6	5,000	2.00%	98.00%	1
Task 9	Manufacturing	50,000	80,000	100,000	207,600	6	9.3	11.5	10,000	20.00%	95.00%	1
Task 10	Reprototyping	8,000	12,000	16,000	29,784	1.6	2.15	2.7	8,000	2.00%	98.00%	1
Task 11	Recasting and rework	12,000	18,000	19,000	35,904	1.6	2.15	2.7	8,000	2.00%	98.00%	1
	Project Total Cost	**99,150**	**151,000**	**193,750**	**377,408**	**25**	**34.65**	**47**	**226,408**			

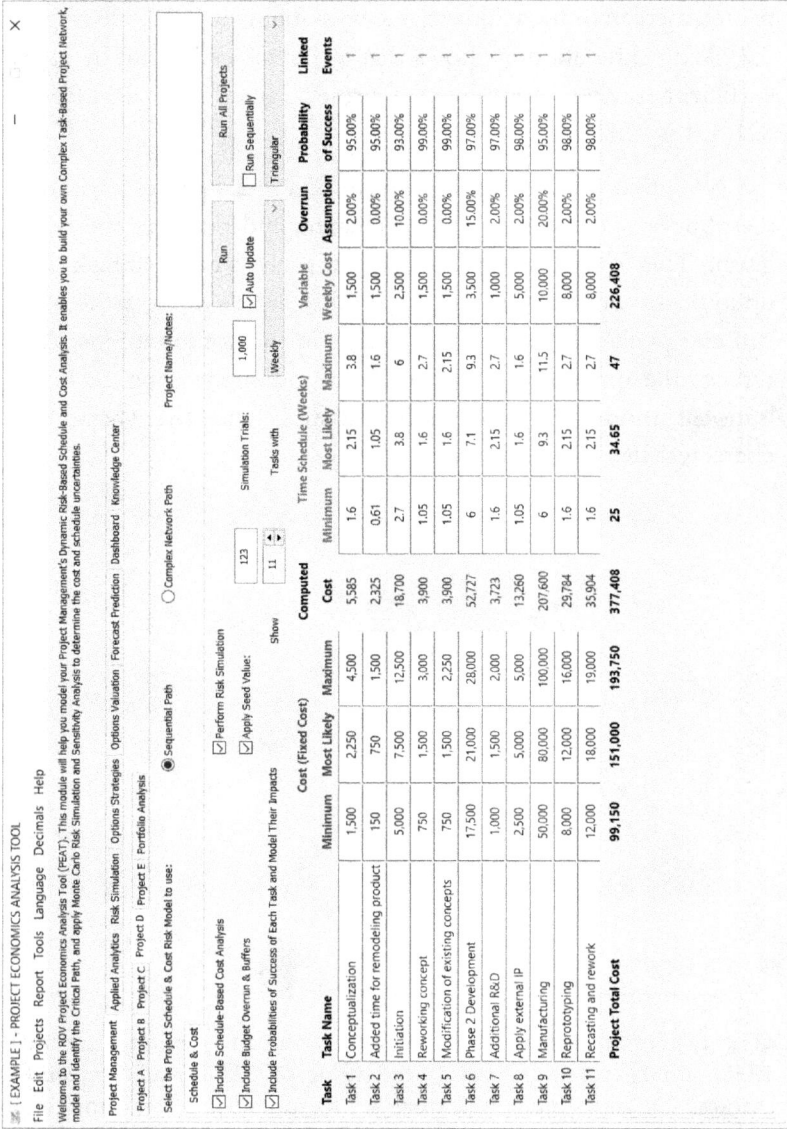

Figure 2.2: Simple Linear Path Project Management with Cost and Schedule Risk

[EXAMPLE] - PROJECT ECONOMICS ANALYSIS TOOL

File   Edit   Projects   Report   Tools   Language   Decimals   Help

Welcome to the ROV Project Economics Analysis Tool (PEAT). This module will help you model your Project Management's Dynamic Risk-Based Schedule and Cost Analysis. It enables you to build your own Complex Task-Based Project Network, model and identify the Critical Path, and apply Monte Carlo Risk Simulation and Sensitivity Analysis to determine the cost and schedule uncertainties.

Project Management   Applied Analytics   Risk Simulation   Options Strategies   Options Valuation   Forecast Prediction   Dashboard   Knowledge Center

Static Tornado   Scenario Analysis

Tornado or static sensitivity analysis is performed by perturbing the inputs a preset amount one at a time to determine the impact on the output variable. Start by selecting the Option and Output Variable to test, then set the sensitivity levels and click Compute to run.

Select the Option and Output Variable to run:

Project D: Expected Project Cost

Sensitivity +/-   10 ⬍ %   Reset
Show the top   10 ⬍ variables
Show results with   2 ⬍ decimals

Select the granularity of the sensitivity analysis:

○ Individual Unique Inputs
○ Line Items
◉ Variable Groups

Update   Excel   🔳 🔳   Copy Chart

The Tornado run has been completed.

Project D: Expected Project Cost

Show results with   2 ⬍ decimals

		Base Value:	377,408.00				Changes		
Chart	% Up	% Down	Inputs	Output Do...	Output Up	Range	Input Do...	Input Up	Base Case
✓	10.00%	10.00%	Task 9	Manufacturing	Time Schedule ...	366,248.00	388,568.00	22,320.00	8.37	10.23	9.30
✓	10.00%	10.00%	Task 9	Manufacturing	Variable Weekl...	366,248.00	388,568.00	22,320.00	9,000.00	11,000.00	10,000.00
✓	10.00%	10.00%	Task 9	Manufacturing	Cost (Fixed Cos...	367,808.00	387,008.00	19,200.00	72,000.00	88,000.00	80,000.00
✓	10.00%	10.00%	Task 6	Phase 2 Development	Time Sc...	374,550.25	380,265.75	5,715.50	6.39	7.81	7.10
✓	10.00%	10.00%	Task 6	Phase 2 Development	Variabl...	374,550.25	380,265.75	5,715.50	3,150.00	3,850.00	3,500.00

Project D: Expected Project Cost

Time Schedule (Weeks) Most Likely   8.37   10.23
Variable Weekly Cost   9,000.00   11,000
Cost (Fixed Cost) Most Likely   72,000   56,000
Time Schedule (Weeks) Most Likely   6.39   7.81
Variable Weekly Cost   3,150.00   3,850.00
Cost (Fixed Cost) Most Likely   18,900   23,100
Variable Weekly Cost   16,200   19,800
Cost (Fixed Cost) Most Likely   7,200.00   8,390.00
Time Schedule (Weeks) Most Likely   1.94   2.37
Time Schedule (Weeks) Most Likely   1.94   2.37

366.000   370.000   375.000   380.000   385.000   390.000

Name:

New   Model
Save As   Proj. A's Cost
           Proj. B's Critical Path
Edit   Proj. D's Schedule
Save   Proj. E's Variable Cost
Delete

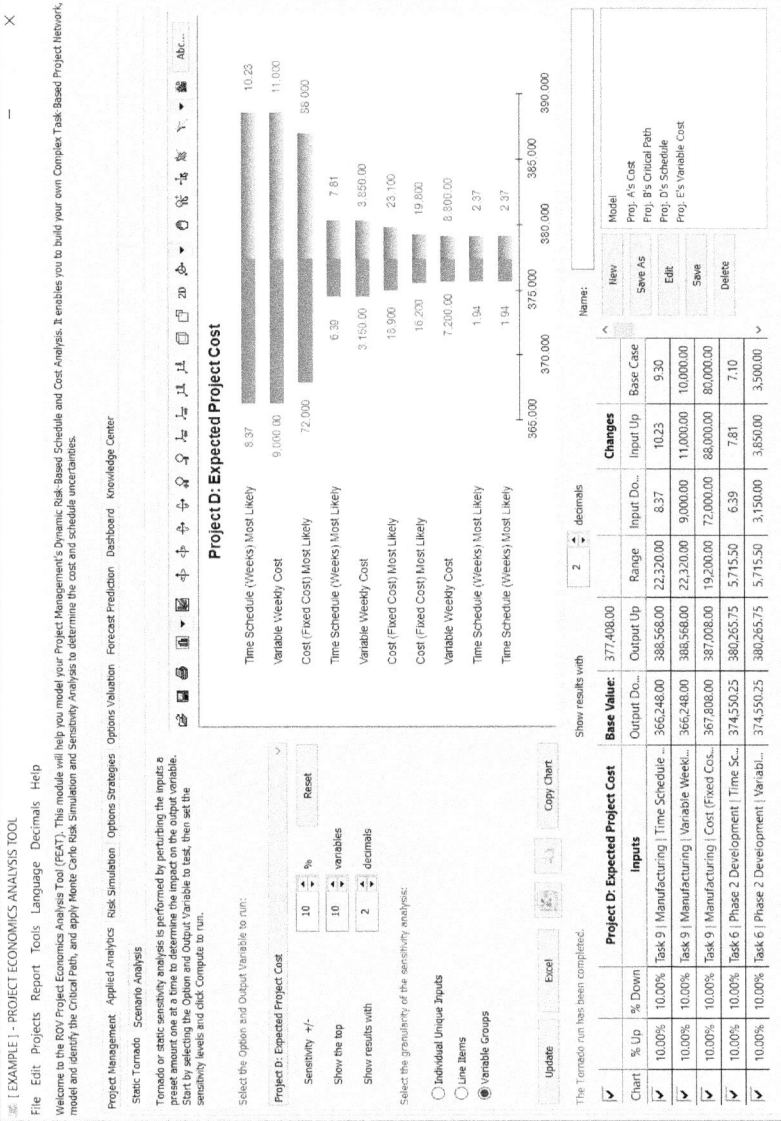

Figure 2.3: Simple Linear Path Tornado Analysis

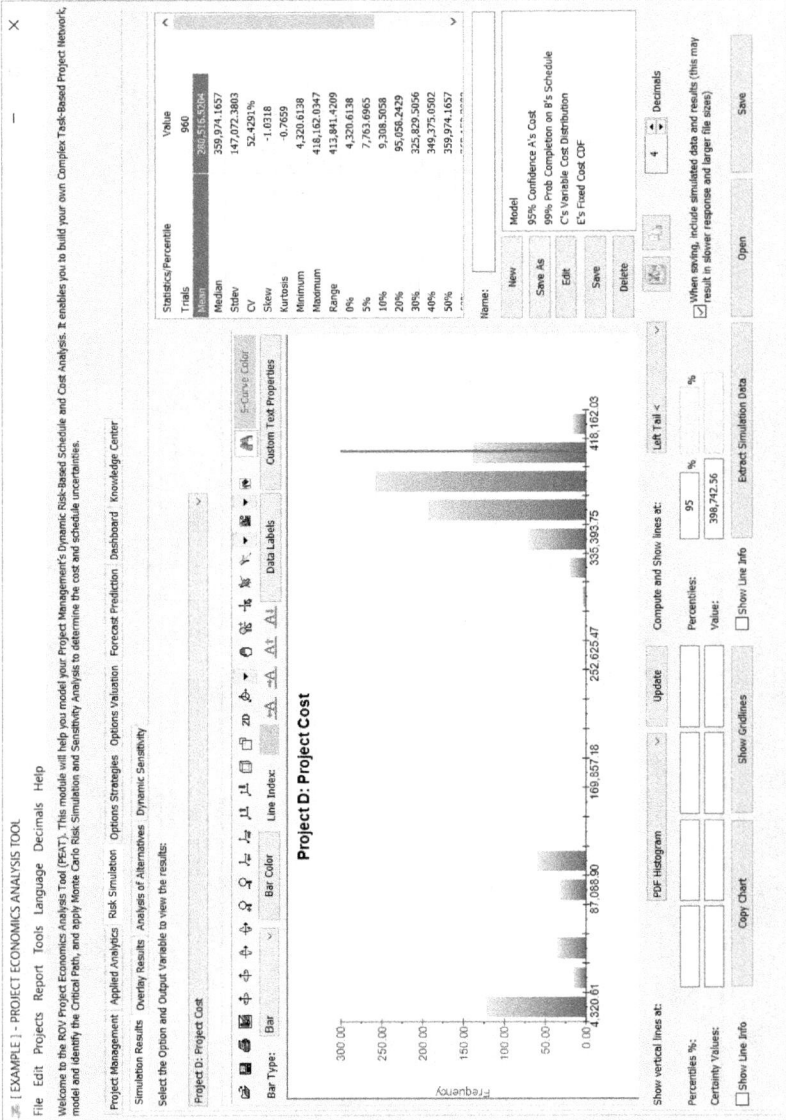

Figure 2.4: Monte Carlo Risk Simulated Results for Risky Cost and Schedule Values

In complex projects where there are nonlinear bifurcating and re-combining paths (Figure 2.5), the cost and schedule risk modeling is more difficult to model and compute. For instance, in the *Project A* tab of the default example, we can see that after Task 1, future tasks can be run in parallel (Tasks 2, 3, and 4). Then, Tasks 3 and 4 recombine into Task 8. Such complex path models can be created by the user simply by adding tasks and combining them in the visual map as shown, using the relevant icon tools (Figure 2.6). The software will automatically create the analytical financial model when *Create Model* is clicked. That is, you will be taken to the *Schedule & Cost* tab and the same setup as shown previously is now available for data entry for this complex model (Figure 2.7). The complex mathematical connections will automatically be created behind the scenes to run the calculations so that the user will only need to perform the very simple tasks of drawing the complex network path connections. Below are some tips on getting started:

- Start by adding a new project if required, from the *Projects* menu. Then, click on the *Complex Network Path* radio selection to access the *Network Diagram* tab.

- Use the icons to assist in drawing your network path. Hover your mouse over the icons to see their descriptions. You can start by clicking on the third icon to *Create a New Task*, and then click anywhere in the drawing canvas to insert said task.

- With an existing task clicked on and selected, click on the fourth icon to *Add a Subtask*. This will automatically create the adjoining next task and next task number. You then need to move this newly inserted task to its new position. Continue with this process as required to create your network diagram. You can create multiple subtasks off a single existing task if simultaneous implementations occur. Simply drag the newly created task box to the desired location.

- Double click on any task node to change its properties such as adding a task name or changing its color.

- When the network diagram is complete, click on *Create Model* to generate the computational algorithms wherein you can then enter the requisite data in the *Schedule & Cost* tab as described previously.

- The icon taskbar shown in Figure 2.6 will come in handy when creating your own custom complex diagram.

    o *Create New Network Model* icon will clear the existing diagram and allow you to start from scratch.

    o *Edit Existing Model* icon is the same as the Edit Model button to the right. It allows you to unlock an existing model to make modifications to it. When done, make sure to click on Save Changes so that the model changes are updated and the algorithmic links between tasks are updated (this will also update the calculations in the *Schedule & Cost* tab).

    o *Add a New Task* icon will add the first task (Task 1) in the canvas area.

    o *Add a New Connected Task* icon will add a new subsequent task, and the link will depend on which task you have currently selected prior to clicking this icon. Note that this icon will not work unless an existing task node is first selected.

    o *Link Task* and *Delete Link* icons are used when you want to add or delete links between task nodes. You can recombine different tasks or merge tasks by clicking on one task, then holding down the control (Ctrl) key and clicking on the second task you wish to join and then clicking on the *Link Tasks* icon to join then. Similarly, you can click on the sixth icon to *Delete Link* between any two tasks.

o *Insert Text or Note Box* icon will insert a text box depending on where you click on the canvas. You can resize the text box and double click on it to insert your own custom text. These text boxes are helpful as they are used to provide added information to the visual model.

o *Undo* and *Redo* icons will simply undo or redo the last command or function.

o *Zoom In* and *Zoom Out* icons allow you to change the zoom on the complex diagram you have created for a better visual.

o *Change Location of Task Name* icon will change the location of where the text of a certain selected task node will appear. This icon will toggle among the four possible text locations around a task node.

o *Change Location of Line Link* icon will toggle among the possible locations where the incoming connection line can be placed. Sometimes, depending on the model created, this change link location may not provide any additional options other than the single location that currently exists.

o *Font Settings* icon will pop up the standard font settings for you to choose, but only if the required task node is first selected. Font settings are specific to each task node.

o *Change Background Size* icon allows you to change the size of the canvas for creating your complex model. The default size is 1361 × 624 pixels.

o *Insert Intermediate Node* icon allows you to insert a floating task node and number it between the starting task and the last task that currently exists. It will then shift all subsequent task numbers appropriately. For example, if your model has Tasks 1–5 set up, you can now insert an intermediate Task 3, and the existing Tasks 3, 4, and 5 will be renumbered to Tasks 4, 5, and 6. You can now select any two tasks by holding down the Ctrl key and clicking on the fifth icon to link the tasks. Note that you may need to manually delete any incorrect links that may now still exist as you add a new intermediate task. Also, any task links automatically detected as invalid will be deleted.

o *Delete Intermediate Node* icon allows you to delete any existing intermediate node. Simply select the task node you wish to delete and click on this icon to delete the node.

o *Renumber Intermediate Node* icon is used to renumber a selected task node. Note that incorrectly linked tasks will now have their links automatically deleted. In addition, by renumbering nodes, you may now need to manually add or delete any links between intermediate nodes as required in your model.

o *Auto Renumber All Nodes* icon will automatically renumber all task nodes at once after intermediate nodes are added or deleted. This function will renumber the nodes consecutively, avoiding any missing intermediate integer values.

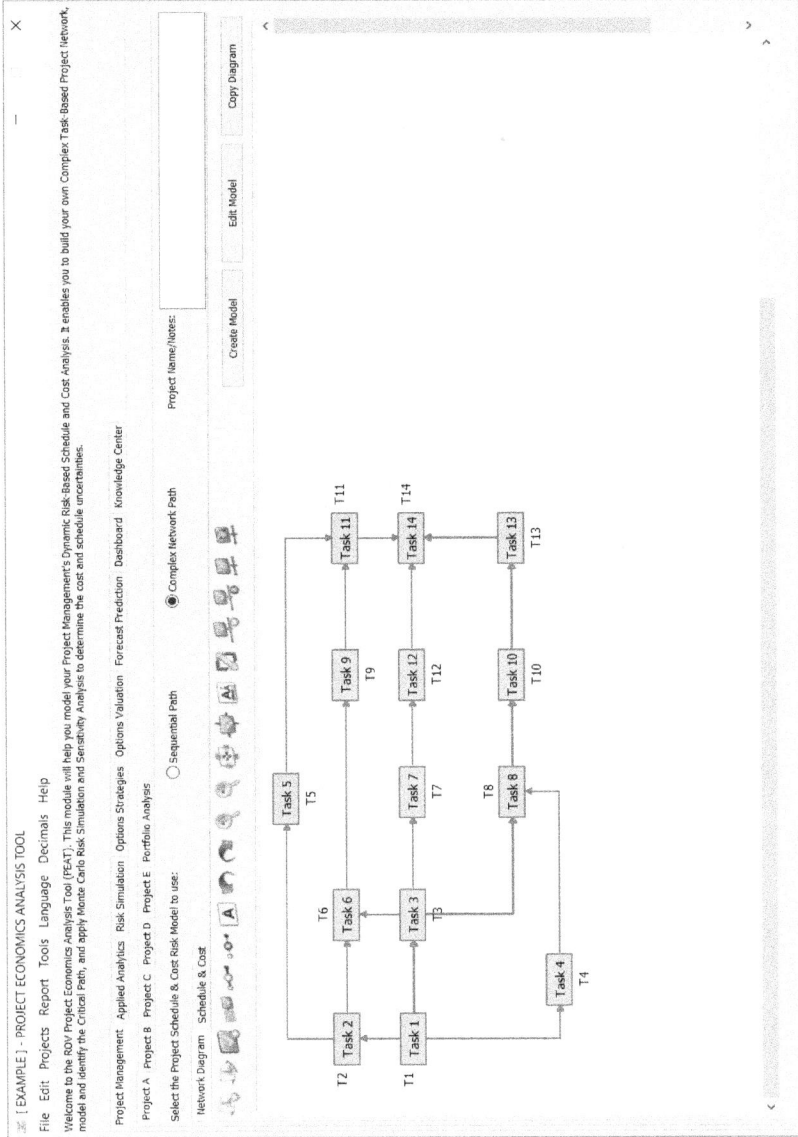

Figure 2.5: Complex Path Project Management

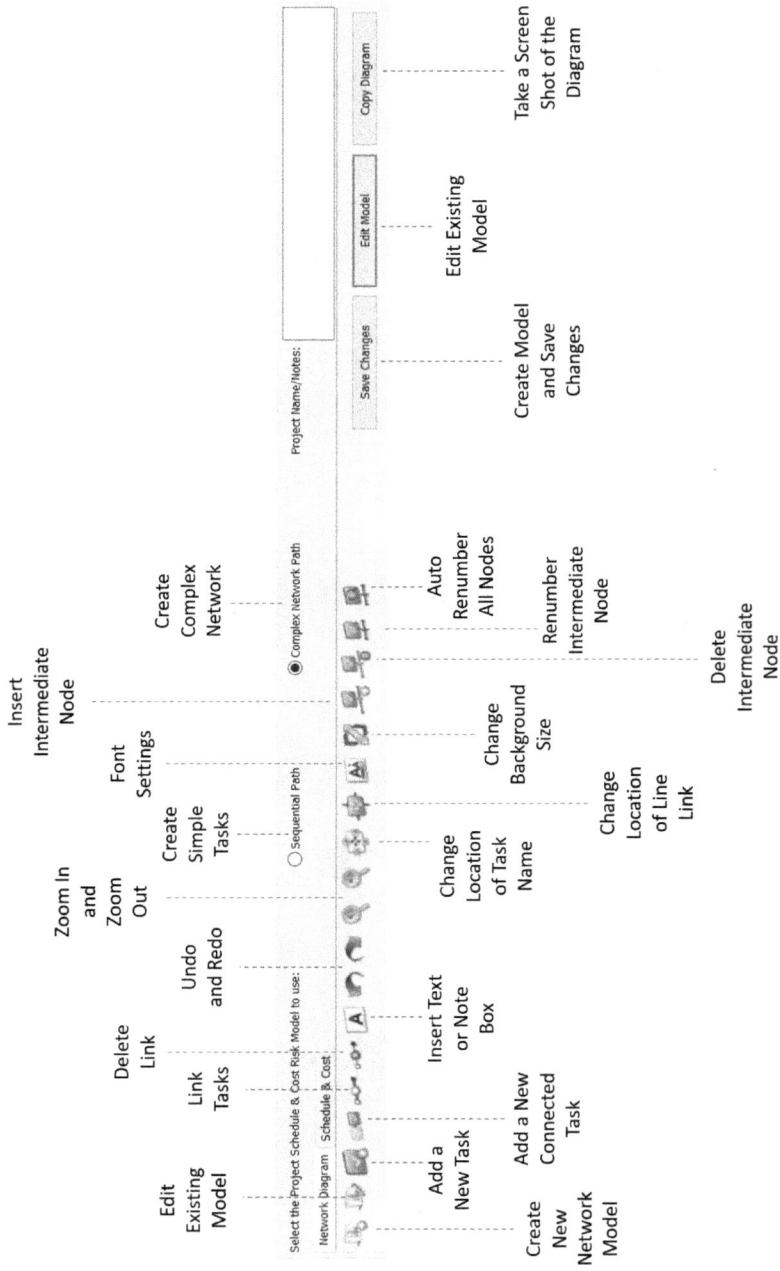

Figure 2.6: Complex Model Icons

File   Edit   Projects   Report   Tools   Language   Decimals   Help

Welcome to the ROV Project Economics Analysis Tool (PEAT). This module will help you model your Project Management's Dynamic Risk-Based Schedule and Cost Analysis. It enables you to build your own Complex Task-Based Project Network, model and identify the Critical Path, and apply Monte Carlo Risk Simulation and Sensitivity Analysis to determine the cost and schedule uncertainties.

Project Management   Applied Analytics   Risk Simulation   Options Strategies   Options Valuation   Forecast Prediction   Dashboard   Knowledge Center

Project A   Project B   Project C   Project D   Project E   Portfolio Analysis

Select the Project Schedule & Cost Risk Model to use: ○ Sequential Path   ● Complex Network Path   Project Name/Notes:

Network Diagram   Schedule & Cost

☑ Include Schedule-Based Cost Analysis   ☑ Perform Risk Simulation   Simulation Trials: 123   Run   Run All Projects

☐ Include Budget Overrun & Buffers   ☑ Apply Seed Value: Tasks with   14 ⬍   ☐ Auto Update   ☐ Run Sequentially

☐ Include Probabilities of Success of Each Task and Model Their Impacts   Show   Weekly ⌄   Triangular ⌄

Task	Task Name	Cost (Fixed Cost)			Computed	Time Schedule (Weeks)			Variable
		Minimum	Most Likely	Maximum	Cost	Minimum	Most Likely	Maximum	Weekly Cost
Task 1	T1	34	39	47	800	34	39	47	19.5
Task 2	T2	17	32	37	544	17	32	37	16
Task 3	T3	21	41	48	882	21	41	48	20.5
Task 4	T4	24	27	36	392	24	27	36	13.5
Task 5	T5	25	32	34	544	25	32	34	16
Task 6	T6	29	35	46	648	29	35	46	17.5
Task 7	T7	31	37	37	722	31	37	37	18.5
Task 8	T8	14	20	24	220	14	20	24	10
Task 9	T9	24	38	39	950	30	48	55	19
Task 10	T10	24	38	40	760	24	38	40	19
Task 11	T11	9	12	16	84	9	12	16	6
Task 12	T12	30	31	45	512	30	31	45	15.5
Task 13	T13	40	42	61	924	40	42	48	21
Task 14	T14	16	17	22	162	16	17	22	8.5
	Project Total	**338**	**441**	**532**	**8,141**	**149**	**197.00**	**229**	**7,700**
	Expected Total Duration				**56.50%**				
	Critical Path 1, 3, 8, 10, 13-14				**30.10%**				
	Critical Path 1, 3, 6, 9, 11, 14								

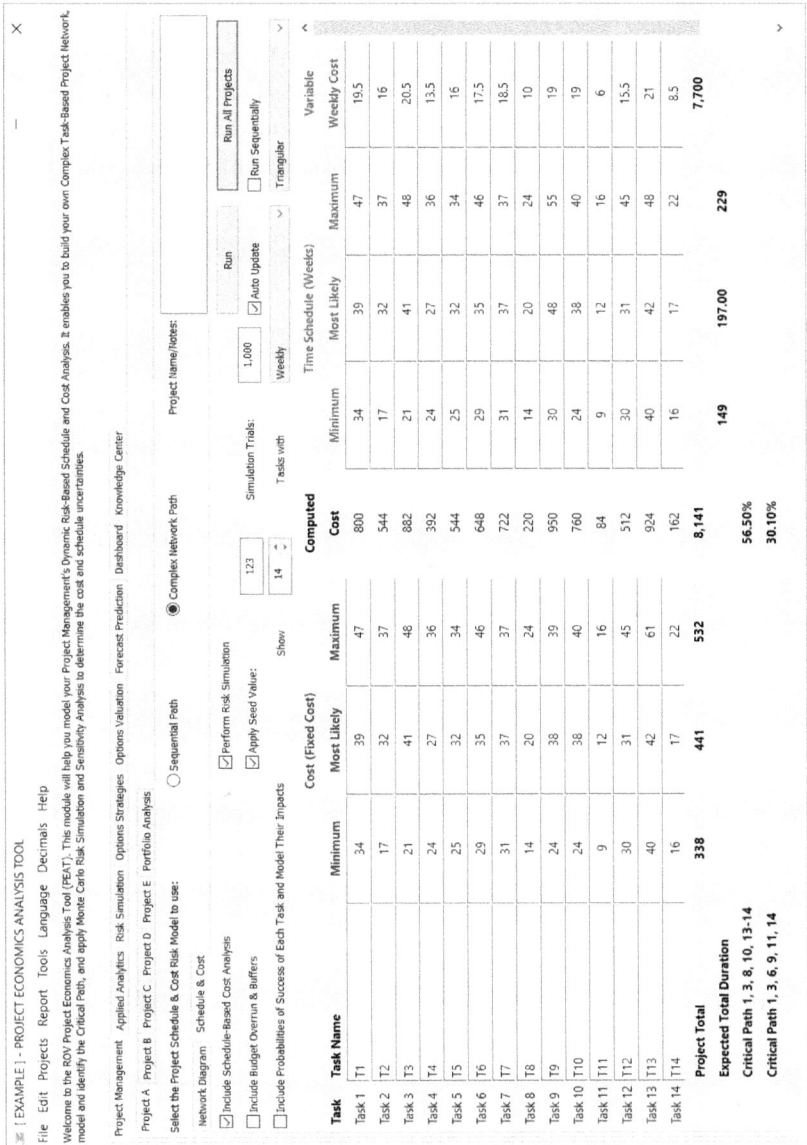

Figure 2.7: Complex Project Simulated Cost and Duration Model with Critical Path

After running the model, the complex path map shows the high-lighted critical path (Figure 2.8) of the project, that is, the path that has the highest potential for bottlenecks and delays in completing the project on time. The exact path specifications and probabilities of being on the critical path is seen in Figure 2.7 (e.g., there is a 56.30% probability that the critical path will be along Tasks 1, 3, 8, 10, 13, 14).

If there are multiple projects or potential project path implementations, the portfolio view (Figure 2.9) compares all projects and implementation paths for the user to make a better and more informed risk-based decision. The simulated distributions can also be overlaid (Figure 2.10) for comparison.

Figure 2.9 allows users to see all projects that were modeled at a glance. Each project modeled can actually be different projects or the same project modeled under different assumptions and implementation options (i.e., different ways of executing the project), to see which project or implementation option path makes more sense in terms of cost and schedule risks. The *Analysis of Alternatives* radio selected allows users to see each project as stand-alone (as compared to *Incremental Analysis* where one of the projects is selected as the base case and all other projects' results show their differences from the base case) in terms of cost and schedule: single-point estimate values, simulated averages, the probabilities that each of the projects will have a cost or schedule overrun, and the 90th percentile value of cost and schedule. Of course, more detailed analysis can be obtained from the *Risk Simulation | Simulation Results* tab, where users can view all of the simulation statistics and select any confidence and percentile values to show. This *Portfolio Analysis* tab also charts the simulated cost and schedule values using bubble and bar charts for a visual representation of the key results.

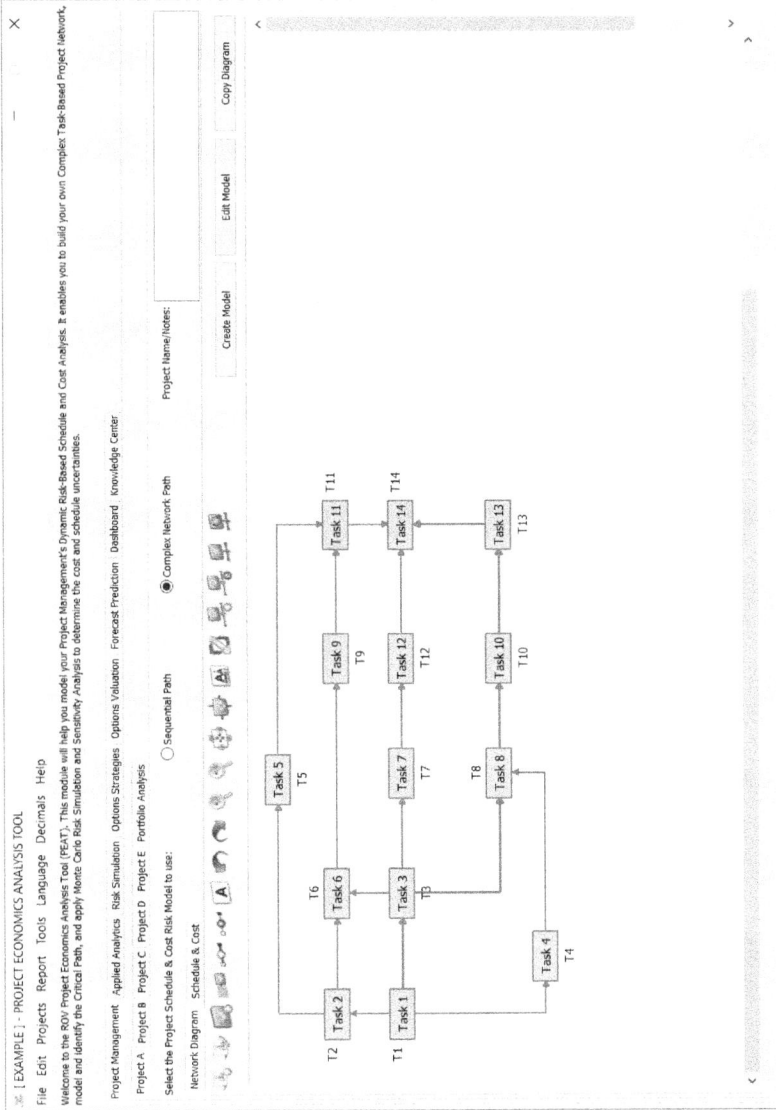

Figure 2.8: Complex Project Critical Path

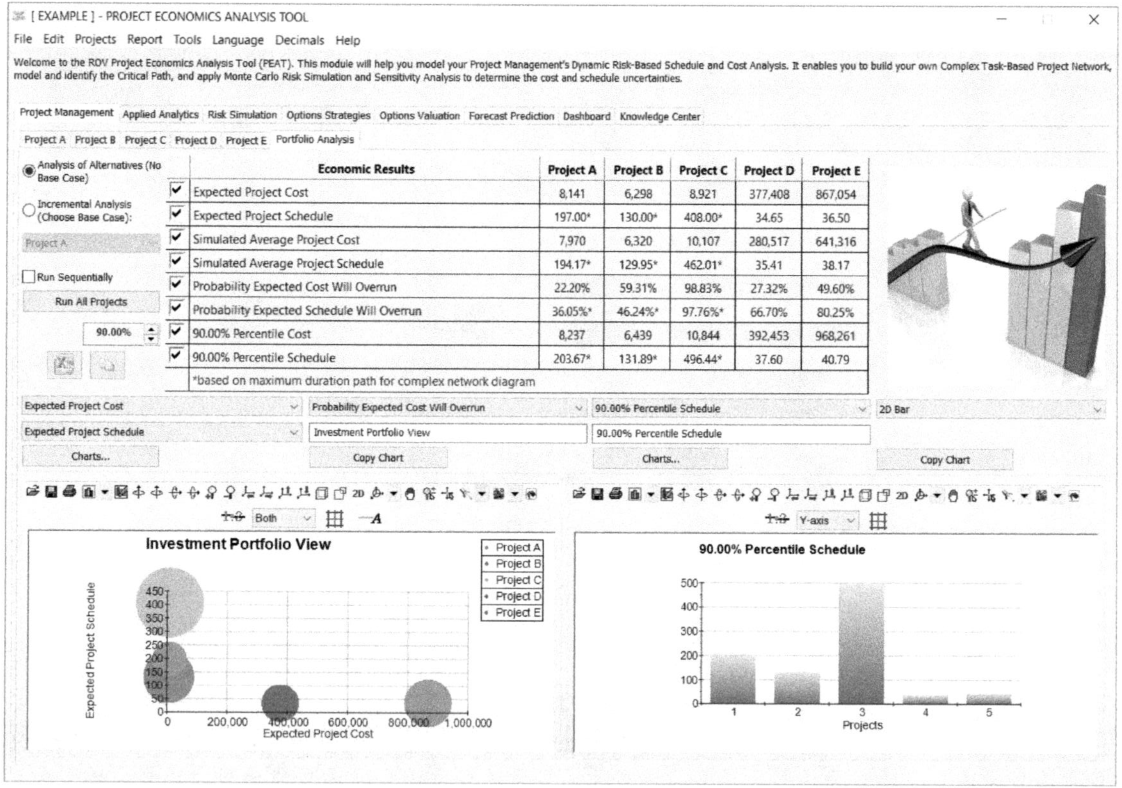
[EXAMPLE] - PROJECT ECONOMICS ANALYSIS TOOL
File Edit Projects Report Tools Language Decimals Help
Welcome to the ROV Project Economics Analysis Tool (PEAT). This module will help you model your Project Management's Dynamic Risk-Based Schedule and Cost Analysis. It enables you to build your own Complex Task-Based Project Network, model and identify the Critical Path, and apply Monte Carlo Risk Simulation and Sensitivity Analysis to determine the cost and schedule uncertainties.
Project Management Applied Analytics Risk Simulation Options Strategies Options Valuation Forecast Prediction Dashboard Knowledge Center
Project A Project B Project C Project D Project E Portfolio Analysis
Analysis of Alternatives (No Base Case)
Incremental Analysis (Choose Base Case):
Project A
Run Sequentially
Run All Projects
90.00%
Economic Results
Project A
Project B
Project C
Project D
Project E
Expected Project Cost 8,141 6,298 8,921 377,408 867,054
Expected Project Schedule 197.00* 130.00* 408.00* 34.65 36.50
Simulated Average Project Cost 7,970 6,320 10,107 280,517 641,316
Simulated Average Project Schedule 194.17* 129.95* 462.01* 35.41 38.17
Probability Expected Cost Will Overrun 22.20% 59.31% 98.83% 27.32% 49.60%
Probability Expected Schedule Will Overrun 36.05%* 46.24%* 97.76%* 66.70% 80.25%
90.00% Percentile Cost 8,237 6,439 10,844 392,453 968,261
90.00% Percentile Schedule 203.67* 131.89* 496.44* 37.60 40.79
*based on maximum duration path for complex network diagram
Expected Project Cost
Expected Project Schedule
Charts...
Probability Expected Cost Will Overrun
Investment Portfolio View
Copy Chart
90.00% Percentile Schedule
90.00% Percentile Schedule
Charts...
2D Bar
Copy Chart
Both
Y-axis
Investment Portfolio View
Expected Project Schedule
Expected Project Cost
0 200,000 400,000 600,000 800,000 1,000,000
Project A
Project B
Project C
Project D
Project E
90.00% Percentile Schedule
Projects
1 2 3 4 5

Figure 2.9: Portfolio View of Multiple Projects at Once

Comparing and Overlaying
Simulated Results

The *Overlay* chart in Figure 2.10 shows multiple projects' simulated costs or schedules overlaid on top of one another to see their relative spreads, location, and skew of the results. We clearly see that the project whose distribution lies to the right has a much higher cost to complete than the left, with the project on the right also having a slightly higher level of uncertainty in terms of cost spreads. Refer to the appendices for more details on interpreting these PDF and CDF charts, as well as on how to make better-informed decisions using their results.

Finally, Figure 2.11 shows an *Analysis of Alternatives* comparison of the simulated results of the projects. While Figure 2.9 shows the expected value of the project costs and schedule (not simulated, static, single-point estimates), Figure 2.11 shows the simulated results.

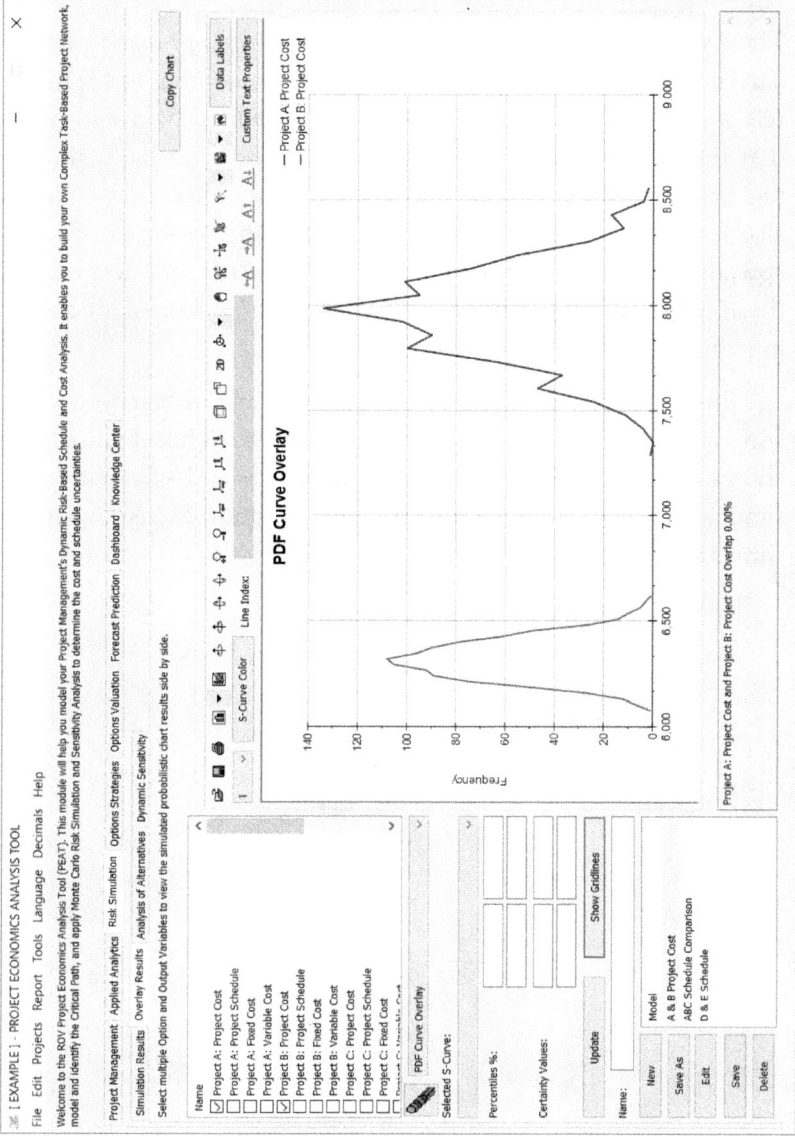

Figure 2.10: Overlay Charts of Multiple Projects' Cost or Schedule

Welcome to the ROV Project Economics Analysis Tool (PEAT). This module will help you model your Project Management's Dynamic Risk-Based Schedule and Cost Analysis. It enables you to build your own Complex Task-Based Project Network, model and identify the Critical Path, and apply Monte Carlo Risk Simulation and Sensitivity Analysis to determine the cost and schedule uncertainties.

Project Management   Applied Analytics   Risk Simulation   Options Strategies   Options Valuation   Forecast Prediction   Dashboard   Knowledge Center

Simulation Results   Overlay Results   Analysis of Alternatives   Dynamic Sensitivity

You can compare the dynamic simulated results of all your options. A simulation must first be run before you can obtain any results. Choose if you wish to compare all options as standalone (Analysis of Alternatives) or against a base case (Incremental Analysis).

ANALYSIS OF ALTERNATIVES AND BASE CASE INCREMENTAL ANALYSIS

◉ Analysis of Alternatives (No Base Case)   ○ Incremental Analysis (Choose Base Case):

Economic Results: Project Cost

OPTIONS	Project A	Project B	Project C	Project D	Project E
◉ Mean	7,969.80	6,319.84	10,106.84	280,516.52	641,316.48
○ Median	7,975.76	6,318.77	10,088.57	359,974.17	865,503.78
○ Stdev	217.63	89.86	549.42	147,072.38	378,791.00
○ Variance	47,316.04	8,067.15	301,564.86	2.16E+010	1.43E+011
○ CV	2.73%	1.42%	5.44%	52.43%	59.06%
○ Skew	-0.1588	0.0228	0.1576	-1.0318	-0.7408
○ Kurtosis	-0.1503	-0.1117	-0.0871	-0.7659	-1.2222
○ Minimum	7,267.61	6,017.59	8,344.81	4,320.61	4,657.65
○ Maximum	8,615.23	6,619.47	11,883.02	418,162.03	1,071,281.34
○ Range	1,347.62	601.88	3,538.21	413,841.42	1,066,623.69
○ 0% Percentile	7,267.61	6,017.59	8,344.81	4,320.61	4,657.65
○ 5% Percentile	7,599.83	6,176.38	9,236.02	7,763.70	6.68412
○ 10% Percentile	7,694.77	6,204.64	9,448.04	9,308.51	8,854.74
○ 20% Percentile	7,783.07	6,245.29	9,638.67	95,058.24	101,378.61
○ 30% Percentile	7,858.54	6,271.69	9,784.60	325,829.51	365,619.43
○ 40% Percentile	7,914.68	6,296.88	9,915.63	349,375.05	821,576.92
○ 50% Percentile	7,975.76	6,318.77	10,088.57	359,974.17	865,503.78
○ 60% Percentile	8,038.75	6,341.98	10,237.34	368,158.21	892,746.63
○ 70% Percentile	8,098.10	6,364.55	10,401.58	375,032.36	917,246.92
○ 80% Percentile	8,153.74	6,397.14	10,579.60	383,463.98	941,854.82
○ 90% Percentile	8,236.72	6,438.69	10,844.00	392,453.01	968,261.01
○ 95% Percentile	8,315.28	6,468.86	11,038.94	398,742.56	990,846.42
○ 100% Percentile	8,615.23	6,619.47	11,883.02	418,162.03	1,071,281.34

Project A
2 ⊕ Decimals

2D Bar   Copy Chart

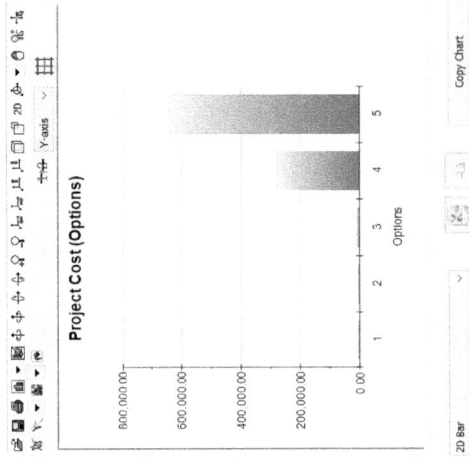

Figure 2.11: Analysis of Alternatives

SCHEDULE & COST
RISK COMPUTATIONS

This chapter showcases a complex task model and its manual computations to determine schedule and cost risk. The model illustrated in Figure 3.1 is a complex schedule network model for the project shown to the right with 24 tasks (nodes). The network is represented in the Activity-On-Node design. The nodes in the network correspond to each project task shown in the figure. The arrows in the figure indicate the precedence relationships between the tasks. A schedule model can be developed by assigning an input assumption for each task, representing the likelihood of completing the particular task at a specific duration. Typically, a triangular distribution is assigned to each activity using three parameters: 1) the minimum time to complete an activity, 2) the most likely time to complete an activity, and 3) the expected maximum time to complete an activity. One must next determine the beginning of the network, the end of the network and any merge points. Merge points are where different paths come together. In the illustration, Task 12 and Task 18 are merge points. The beginning and end can be considered pseudo-merge points. You will then create formulas to calculate the durations of the various paths from merge point to merge point and retain the longest (maximum) duration path as the subtotal duration for that part of the network.

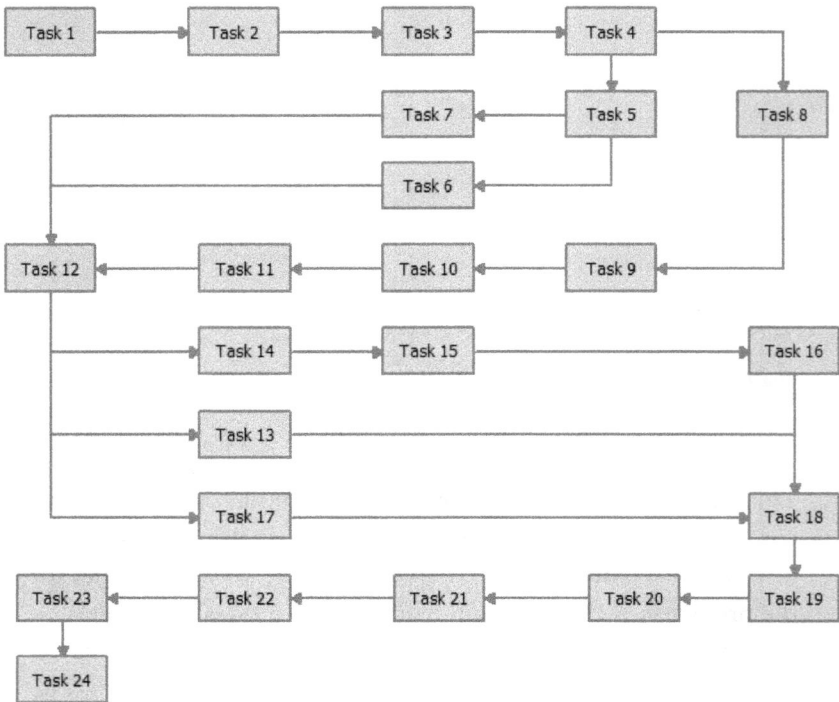

Figure 3.1: Sample Complex Task Model

Schedule Risk

In Figure 3.2, the sample schedule inputs in days are shown. In order to illustrate the step-by-step computations, we will use an Excel worksheet grid.

The first subtotal sums the durations for Tasks 1 through 4 (Tasks 1–4). The next subtotal is the maximum duration of the paths Tasks 5&6, Task 5&7, and Tasks 8–11. The third subtotal is the duration of Task 12. The fourth subtotal is the maximum duration of Task 13, Tasks 14-16, and Task 17. The last subtotal sums the duration for the remaining tasks (Tasks 18–24). The sum of the subtotals is the forecast for the complete schedule. When you run the model, you will get a forecast for the entire range of possible durations for the entire project.

	A	B	C	D	E	F
1			Duration			
2		Task	MIN	ML	MAX	Simulation
3		T1	2	5	10	5.00
4		T2	5	10	15	10.00
5		T3	30	45	90	45.00
6		T4	5	10	15	10.00
7		T5	30	45	90	45.00
8		T6	5	10	15	10.00
9		T7	15	25	60	25.00
10		T8	10	20	60	20.00
11		T9	5	15	30	15.00
12		T10	5	10	15	10.00
13		T11	15	25	45	25.00
14		T12	15	20	30	20.00
15		T13	20	30	45	30.00
16		T14	30	45	60	45.00
17		T15	15	30	45	30.00
18		T16	5	10	20	10.00
19		T17	10	15	25	15.00
20		T18	15	30	60	30.00
21		T19	10	15	30	15.00
22		T20	15	30	60	30.00
23		T21	5	10	15	10.00
24		T22	30	60	90	60.00
25		T23	5	10	15	10.00
26		T24	5	8	12	8.00

Figure 3.2: Sample Schedule Inputs

- Subtotal 1 = 70.00
    - SUM(F3:F6) or 5 + 10 + 45 + 10 = 70
    - Sum of duration for Tasks 1–4
- Subtotal 2 = 70.00
    - MAX(SUM(F7:F8),SUM(F7,F9),SUM(F10:F13)) or MAX(45+10, 45+25, 20+15+10+25) = 70
    - Maximum of (Tasks 5 & 6, Tasks 5 & 7, Tasks 8–11)
- Subtotal 3 = 20.00
    - F14 or 20
    - Duration of Task 12
- Subtotal 4 = 85.00
    - MAX(F15,SUM(F16:F18),F19) or MAX(30, 45 + 30 + 10, 15) = 85
    - Maximum of (Task 13, Task 14–16, Task 17)
- Subtotal 5 = 163.00
    - SUM(F20:F26) or 30 + 15 + 30 + 10 + 60 + 10 + 8 = 163
    - Sum of duration of Tasks 18–24
- TOTAL = 408.00
    - 70 + 70 + 20 + 85 + 163 = 408
    - Output Forecast schedule for entire network

Cost Risk

Figure 3.3 shows some sample inputs for fixed and variable costs.

- Fixed Cost = 36.00
  - $1.5 + 1.5 + \ldots + 1.5 = 36$
- Variable Cost = Unit Cost × Simulated Schedule Duration
  - $0.2 \times 5 + 0.2 \times 10 + \ldots + 0.2 \times 8 = 106.60$
- Total Cost = Fixed Cost + Variable Cost
  - $36.0 + 106.6 = 142.6$

Fixed Cost (FC)					Variable Cost (VC)	
Task	MIN	ML	MAX	Simulation	Unit Cost	Total VC
T1	$1.0	$1.5	$3.0	1.50	$0.2	$1.0
T2	$1.0	$1.5	$3.0	1.50	$0.2	$2.0
T3	$1.0	$1.5	$3.0	1.50	$0.2	$9.0
T4	$1.0	$1.5	$3.0	1.50	$0.2	$2.0
T5	$1.0	$1.5	$3.0	1.50	$0.2	$9.0
T6	$1.0	$1.5	$3.0	1.50	$0.2	$2.0
T7	$1.0	$1.5	$3.0	1.50	$0.2	$5.0
T8	$1.0	$1.5	$3.0	1.50	$0.2	$4.0
T9	$1.0	$1.5	$3.0	1.50	$0.2	$3.0
T10	$1.0	$1.5	$3.0	1.50	$0.2	$2.0
T11	$1.0	$1.5	$3.0	1.50	$0.2	$5.0
T12	$1.0	$1.5	$3.0	1.50	$0.2	$4.0
T13	$1.0	$1.5	$3.0	1.50	$0.2	$6.0
T14	$1.0	$1.5	$3.0	1.50	$0.2	$9.0
T15	$1.0	$1.5	$3.0	1.50	$0.2	$6.0
T16	$1.0	$1.5	$3.0	1.50	$0.2	$2.0
T17	$1.0	$1.5	$3.0	1.50	$0.2	$3.0
T18	$1.0	$1.5	$3.0	1.50	$0.2	$6.0
T19	$1.0	$1.5	$3.0	1.50	$0.2	$3.0
T20	$1.0	$1.5	$3.0	1.50	$0.2	$6.0
T21	$1.0	$1.5	$3.0	1.50	$0.2	$2.0
T22	$1.0	$1.5	$3.0	1.50	$0.2	$12.0
T23	$1.0	$1.5	$3.0	1.50	$0.2	$2.0
T24	$1.0	$1.5	$3.0	1.50	$0.2	$1.6

Sum FC	$24.0	$36.0	$72.0		Sum VC	$106.6
					Total Cost	$142.6

Figure 3.3: Sample Cost Inputs

Using PEAT to Model
Cost and Schedule Risk

Using PEAT's Project Management module, we replicate Figure 3.1's complex model as shown in Figure 3.4. The same approach was used to create the model as previously discussed in Chapter 2. Further, the input assumptions shown in Figures 3.2 and 3.3 have been entered into PEAT (Figures 3.5 and 3.6).

Monte Carlo risk simulation was run, and the critical path probabilities are seen in Figure 3.6 at the bottom of the screen. There are only two probable critical paths, 1–5, 7, 12, 14–16, 18–24 and 1–4, 8–12, 14–16, 18–24. This indicates that the two critical paths are highly similar, except for Tasks 5, 7, and 12 versus 8–12. Further, we see in Figure 3.6 that the total most likely schedule is 408 weeks, and the total fixed costs are $24, $36, $72, with the total cost being $143. These are the exact results from our manual computations in Figures 3.2 and 3.3.

Figure 3.7 shows the main critical path (the one with the highest probability of occurrence), and Figure 3.8 show the simulated schedule has a mean of 458.42 weeks with a 99th percentile value at 519.10 weeks. This means that using a single-point estimate of 408 weeks would yield a completely incorrect assessment of the actual schedule risk. On average, there will be a 50.42-week schedule slip. In the absolute worst-case scenario, we are still sure that, 99% of the time, the project will complete in 519.0 weeks.

Figure 3.9 shows the simulated cost, where the mean is $162.86M with a 90% confidence interval that cost will be between $151.57M and $173.91M. This means that there is 5% chance cost will be below $151.57M and 5% chance it will exceed $173.91M. This is a far cry from the $143M single-point estimate. In this case, there will be an average $19.86M budget overrun. If simulation was not applied, the project would be both significantly overbudget and very late, based on projections.

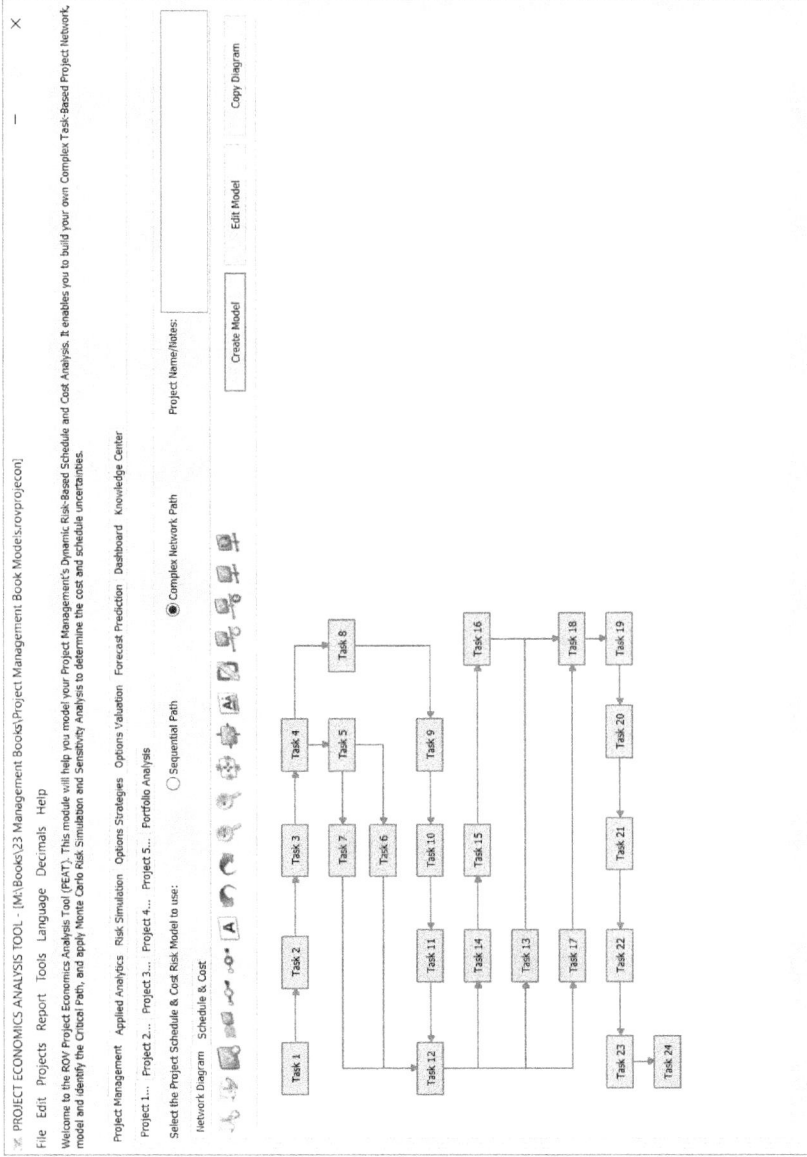

Figure 3.4: PEAT Network Task Diagram

File Edit Projects Report Tools Language Decimals Help

Welcome to the ROV Project Economics Analysis Tool (PEAT). This module will help you model your Project Management's Dynamic Risk-Based Schedule and Cost Analysis. It enables you to build your own Complex Task-Based Project Network, model and identify the Critical Path, and apply Monte Carlo Risk Simulation and Sensitivity Analysis to determine the cost and schedule uncertainties.

Project Management Applied Analytics Risk Simulation Options Strategies Options Valuation Forecast Prediction Dashboard Knowledge Center

Project 1... Project 2... Project 3... Project 4... Project 5... Portfolio Analysis

Select the Project Schedule & Cost Risk Model to use: ○ Sequential Path   ● Complex Network Path   Project Name/Notes:

Network Diagram Schedule & Cost

☑ Include Schedule-Based Cost Analysis   ☑ Perform Risk Simulation   Simulation Trials: Run   Run All Projects
☐ Include Budget Overrun & Buffers   ☑ Apply Seed Value: 123   1,000   ☑ Auto Update   ☐ Run Sequentially
☐ Include Probabilities of Success of Each Task and Model Their Impacts   Tasks with   Show   24   Daily   Triangular

Task	Task Name	Cost (Fixed Cost)			Computed Cost	Time Schedule (Days)			Variable Cost
		Minimum	Most Likely	Maximum		Minimum	Most Likely	Maximum	Daily Cost
Task 1	T1	1.0	1.5	3.0	3	2	5	10	0.2
Task 2	T2	1.0	1.5	3.0	4	5	10	15	0.2
Task 3	T3	1.0	1.5	3.0	11	30	45	90	0.2
Task 4	T4	1.0	1.5	3.0	4	5	10	15	0.2
Task 5	T5	1.0	1.5	3.0	11	30	45	90	0.2
Task 6	T6	1.0	1.5	3.0	4	5	10	15	0.2
Task 7	T7	1.0	1.5	3.0	7	15	25	60	0.2
Task 8	T8	1.0	1.5	3.0	6	10	20	60	0.2
Task 9	T9	1.0	1.5	3.0	5	5	15	30	0.2
Task 10	T10	1.0	1.5	3.0	4	5	10	15	0.2
Task 11	T11	1.0	1.5	3.0	7	15	25	45	0.2
Task 12	T12	1.0	1.5	3.0	6	15	20	30	0.2
Task 13	T13	1.0	1.5	3.0	8	20	30	45	0.2
Task 14	T14	1.0	1.5	3.0	11	30	45	60	0.2
Task 15	T15	1.0	1.5	3.0	8	15	30	45	0.2
Task 16	T16	1.0	1.5	3.0	4	5	10	20	0.2
Task 17	T17	1.0	1.5	3.0	5	10	15	25	0.2
Task 18	T18	1.0	1.5	3.0	8	15	30	60	0.2

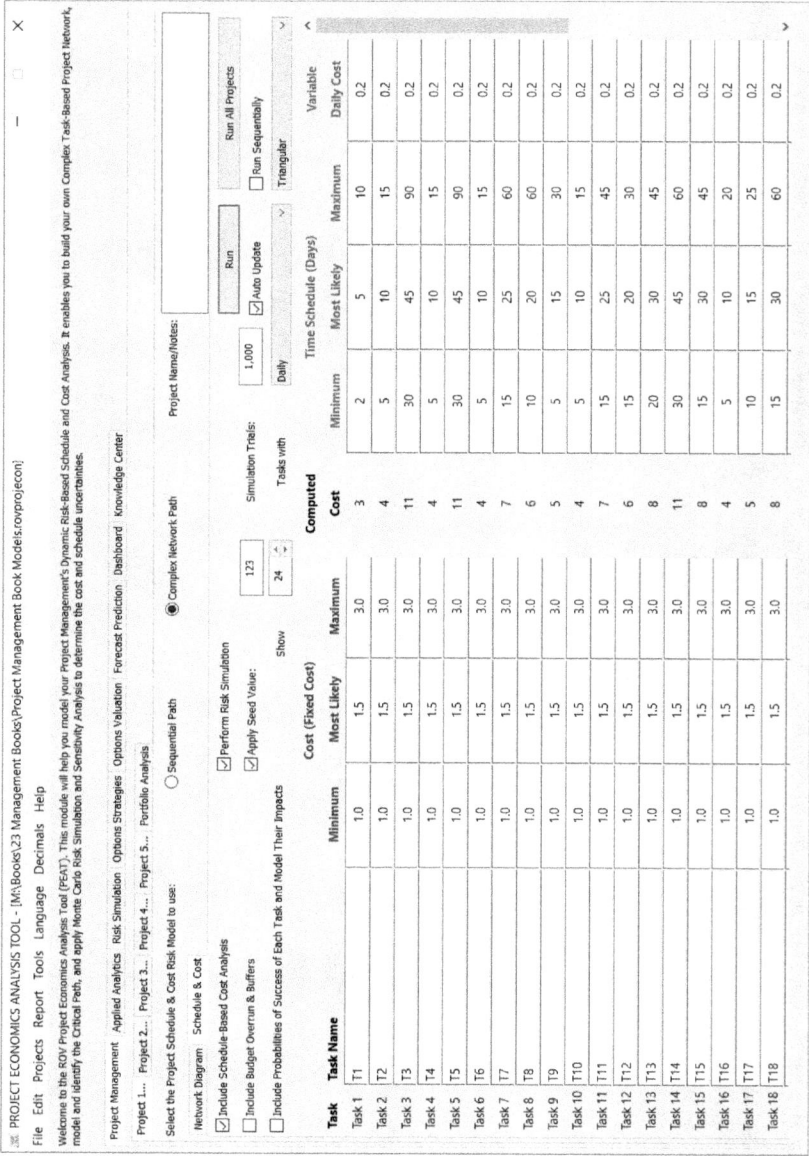

Figure 3.5: Fixed Cost, Schedule, and Variable Cost Inputs

File Edit Projects Report Tools Language Decimals Help

Welcome to the ROV Project Economics Analysis Tool (PEAT). This module will help you model your Project Management's Dynamic Risk-Based Schedule and Cost Analysis. It enables you to build your own Complex Task-Based Project Network model and identify the Critical Path, and apply Monte Carlo Risk Simulation and Sensitivity Analysis to determine the cost and schedule uncertainties.

Project Management | Applied Analytics Risk Simulation Options Strategies Options Valuation Forecast Prediction Dashboard Knowledge Center

Project 1... Project 2... Project 3... Project 4... Project 5... Portfolio Analysis

Select the Project Schedule & Cost Risk Model to use: ○ Sequential Path   ● Complex Network Path   Project Name/Notes:

Network Diagram   Schedule & Cost

☑ Include Schedule-Based Cost Analysis   ☑ Perform Risk Simulation   Simulation Trials: 1,000   Run   Run All Projects
☐ Include Budget Overrun & Buffers   ☑ Apply Seed Value: 123   ☑ Auto Update   ☐ Run Sequentially
☐ Include Probabilities of Success of Each Task and Model Their Impacts   Show 24

Task				Tasks with	Daily		Triangular	
Task 16	T16	1.0	1.5	3.0	4	5	10	20	0.2
Task 17	T17	1.0	1.5	3.0	5	10	15	25	0.2
Task 18	T18	1.0	1.5	3.0	8	15	30	60	0.2
Task 19	T19	1.0	1.5	3.0	5	10	15	30	0.2
Task 20	T20	1.0	1.5	3.0	8	15	30	60	0.2
Task 21	T21	1.0	1.5	3.0	4	5	10	15	0.2
Task 22	T22	1.0	1.5	3.0	14	30	60	90	0.2
Task 23	T23	1.0	1.5	3.0	4	5	10	15	0.2
Task 24	T24	1.0	1.5	3.0	3	5	8	12	0.2
Project Total		**24**	**36**	**72**	**143**	**237**	**408.00**	**717**	**107**

Expected Total Duration

Critical Path	
Critical Path 1-5, 7, 12, 14-16, 18-24	54.20%
Critical Path 1-4, 8-12, 14-16, 18-24	45.80%
Critical Path 1-4, 8-12, 17-24	0.00%
Critical Path 1-5, 7, 12-13, 18-24	0.00%
Critical Path 1-6, 12, 14-16, 18-24	0.00%
Critical Path 1-6, 12, 17-24	0.00%
Critical Path 1-5, 7, 12, 17-24	0.00%
Critical Path 1-4, 8-13, 18-24	0.00%
Critical Path 1-6, 12-13, 18-24	0.00%

Figure 3.6: Simulated Critical Paths

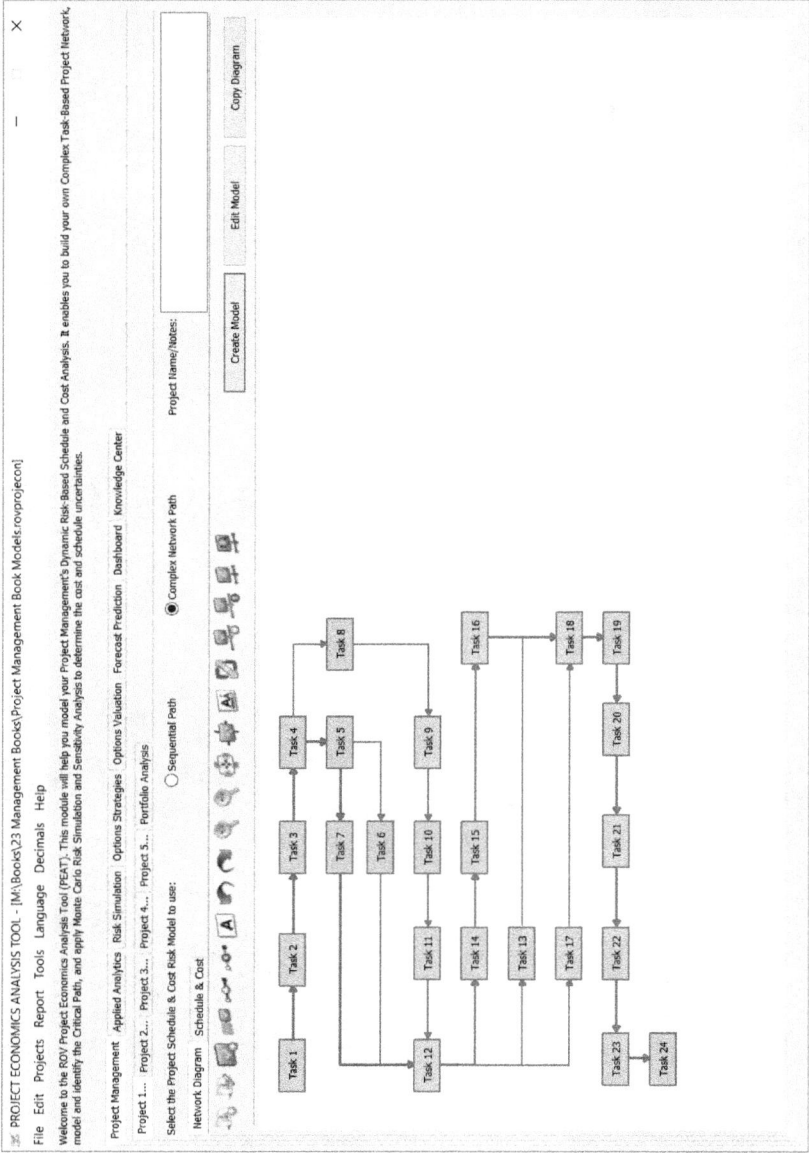

Figure 3.7: Main Critical Path

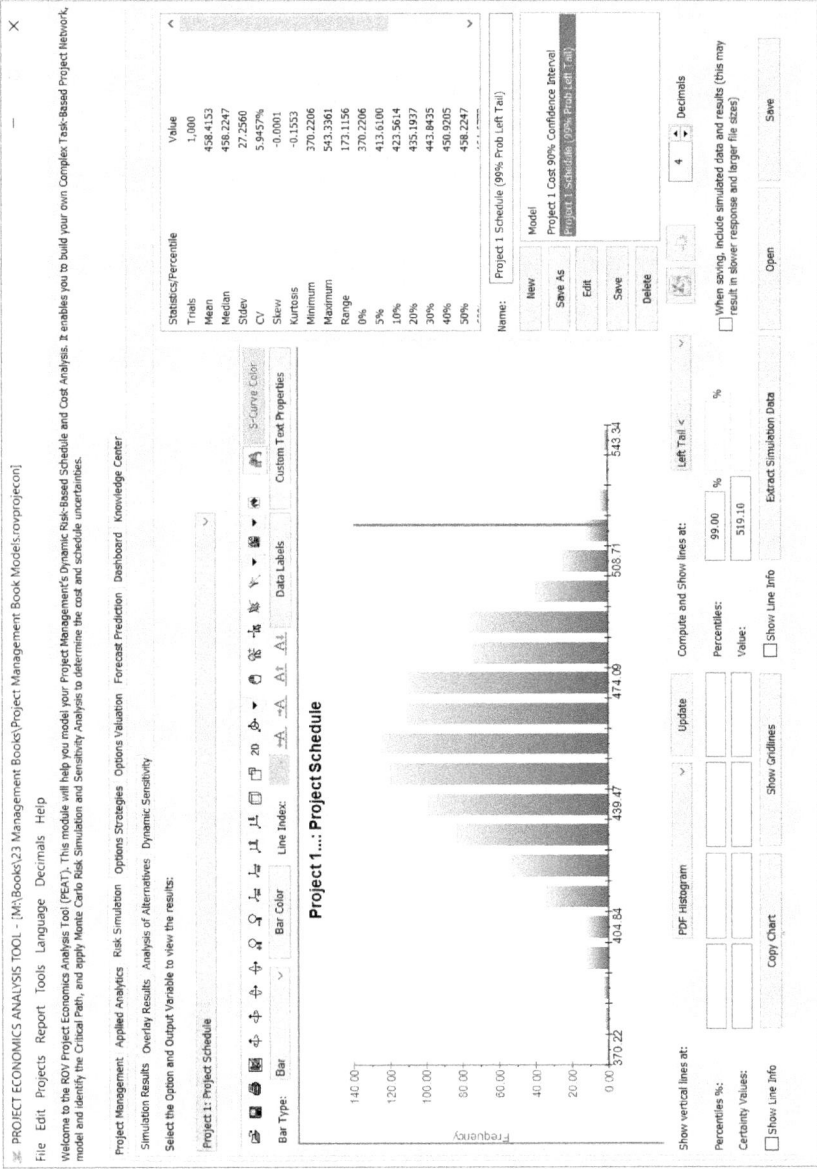

Figure 3.8: Simulated Schedule Risk Profile

File   Edit   Projects   Report   Tools   Language   Decimals   Help

Welcome to the ROV Project Economics Analysis Tool (PEAT). This module will help you model your Project Management's Dynamic Risk-Based Schedule and Cost Analysis. It enables you to build your own Complex Task-Based Project Network, model and identify the Critical Path, and apply Monte Carlo Risk Simulation and Sensitivity Analysis to determine the cost and schedule uncertainties.

Project Management   Applied Analytics   Risk Simulation   Options Strategies   Options Valuation   Forecast Prediction   Dashboard   Knowledge Center

Simulation Results   Overlay Results   Analysis of Alternatives   Dynamic Sensitivity

Select the Option and Output Variable to view the results:

Project 1: Project Cost

Bar Type: Bar   Bar Color   Line Index: Data Labels   Custom Text Properties   S-Curve Color

Project 1...: Project Cost

Frequency axis: 0.00, 20.00, 40.00, 60.00, 80.00, 100.00, 120.00

X-axis: 141.05   149.08   157.11   165.14   173.17   181.20

Statistics/Percentile	Value
Trials	1,000
Mean	162.8565
Median	162.7994
Stdev	6.7812
CV	4.1639%
Skew	-0.1017
Kurtosis	0.1285
Minimum	141.1952
Maximum	181.1952
Range	40.1473
0%	141.0479
5%	151.5663
10%	153.9474
20%	157.4690
30%	159.2214
40%	161.1069
50%	162.7994

Name: Project 1 Cost 90% Confidence Interval

Model
Project 1 Cost 90% Confidence Interval
Project 1 Schedule (99% Prob Left Tail)

New   Save As   Edit   Save   Delete

When saving, include simulated data and results (this may result in slower response and larger file sizes)

Open   Save

Decimals: 4

Show vertical lines at: PDF Histogram   Update   Compute and Show lines at: Two Tails

Percentiles %:   Percentiles: 5.00   %   95.00   %
Certainty Values: Show Gridlines   Value: 151.57   173.91
Show Line Info   Copy Chart   Show Line Info   Extract Simulation Data

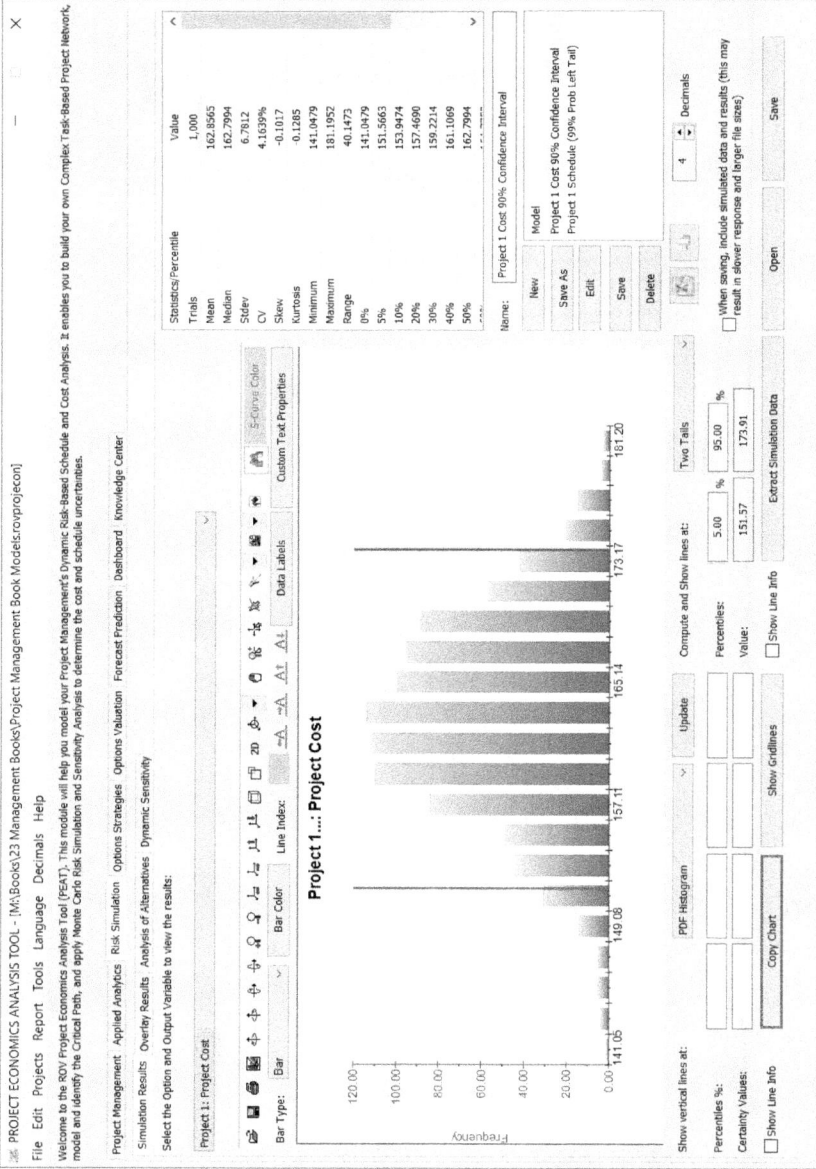

Figure 3.9: Simulated Cost Risk Profile

SCHEDULE SIMULATION

Sometimes, exact dates need to be simulated, instead of the number of months, weeks, or days. This can be done very simply using Excel and Risk Simulator, and we briefly illustrate the approach in this chapter.

Creating and Simulating Schedule Models in Excel

Figure 4.1 shows a simple project timing and schedule calculation. The example shows 5 tasks with subsections or subtasks, with some assumptions of minimum, most likely, and maximum duration measured in weeks. There are also probabilities that a delay or rework is required. The highlighted cells are simulation assumptions and the final date is set as a forecast cell in Risk Simulator. For details on running simulations using Risk Simulator, please refer to Dr. Johnathan Mun's *Modeling Risk*, Third Edition (Thompson–Shore, 2016) or *Readings in Certified Quantitative Risk Management* (IIPER Press, 2016).

Risk-Based Monte Carlo Simulation of Project Management and Timing

Contractual Start Date	30-Jan-20

	Start Date St	Duration in weeks				Finish Date	Probability	Start lag in weeks				Finish lag in weeks			
		Assumption	Min	ML	Max			Assumption	Min	ML	Max	Assumption	Min	ML	Max
CONCEPT PHASE (Task 01)															
Phase Completion	30-Jan-20	18.0	15	18	24	4-Jun-20	90%								
Rework risk	4-Jun-20	3.0	2	3	5	25-Jun-20	10%								
Total (c)						6-Jun-20									
INITIATION (Task 02)															
Phase Completion	30-Jan-20	5.0	3	5	9	5-Mar-20	85%								
Delay risk	5-Mar-20	5.0	3	5	7	9-Apr-20	15%								
Total (c)						10-Mar-20									
DEVELOPMENT (Task 03)															
Phase Completion	6-Jun-20	7.0	6	7	8	25-Jul-20	15%					2.5	1.1	2.5	3.1
MANUFACTURING (Task 04)															
Product A	12-Sep-20	5.0	3	5	7	17-Oct-20	85%	7.0	6	7	8				
Product B	17-Oct-20	4.0	3	4	5	14-Nov-20	10%								
Product C	14-Nov-20	5.0	3	5	9	19-Dec-20	5%								
Customized	19-Dec-20	9.0	4	9	11	18-Feb-18									
GO TO MARKET (Task 05)															
USA															
Product A	7-Nov-20	7.0	6	7	8	26-Dec-20	90%	3.0	1	3	4				
Product B	26-Dec-20	8.0	6	8	9	20-Feb-21									
Product C	20-Feb-21	7.0	6	7	9	10-Apr-21									
Europe															
Product A	7-Nov-20	8.0	7	8	9	2-Jan-21	10%	3.0	2	3	6				
Product B	2-Jan-21	6.0	5	6	10	13-Feb-21									
Product C	13-Feb-21	6.0	4	6	9	27-Mar-21									
Final Completion Date						8-Apr-21									

Date Conversion:	7-May-21
	44323.30

Figure 4.1: Schedule Model with Simulation

Once the simulation is complete, we can determine the risk profile as usual. For example, Figure 4.2 shows that there is a 90% probability that the project will complete by date 44323.30 or May 7, 2021. The simulated risk profile is shown in Figure 4.3. Note that Risk Simulator will run simulations based on a numerical value and will return its results using the same numerical value. Simply enter this number in an empty cell and right-click the cell or CTRL+1 to open the *Format Cells* dialog (Figure 4.4) and change the *Number* formatting to *Custom* dates. The bottom of Figure 4.1 shows both the numerical value and the date conversion using the format cell approach. All other numerical values can be similarly converted into a calendar date.

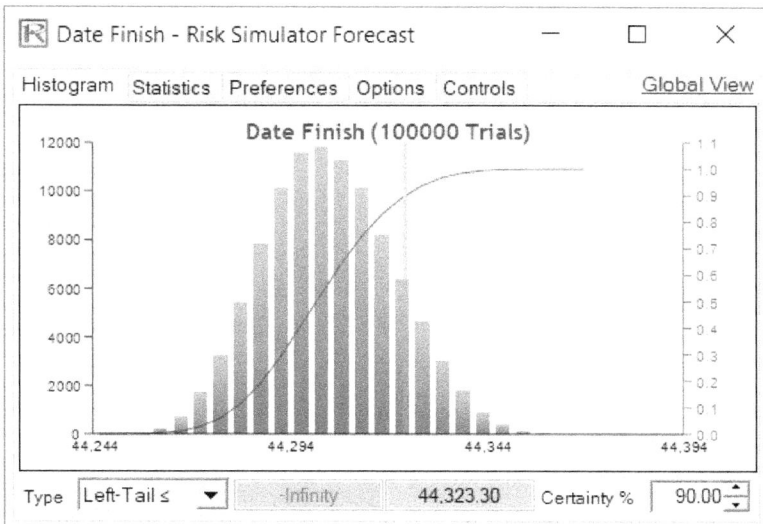

Figure 4.2: Simulated Results – Percentile

Date Finish - Risk Simulator Forecast — □ ✕

Histogram | Statistics | Preferences | Options | Controls — Global View

Statistics	Result
Number of Trials	100000
Mean	44,301.2441
Median	44,300.6298
Standard Deviation	16.5581
Variance	274.1695
Coefficient of Variation	0.0004
Maximum	44,368.4831
Minimum	44,240.5127
Range	127.9704
Skewness	0.1412
Kurtosis	-0.2435
25% Percentile	44,289.5505
75% Percentile	44,312.5190
Percentage Error Precision at 95% C...	0.0002%

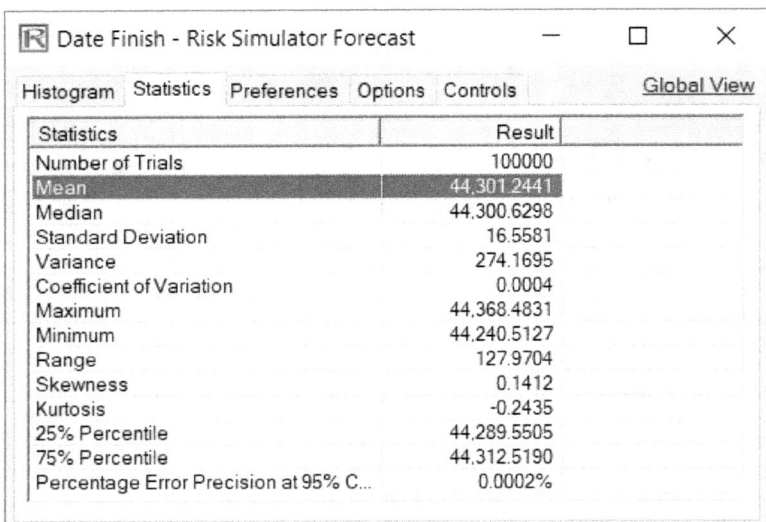

Figure 4.3: Simulated Results – Risk Profile

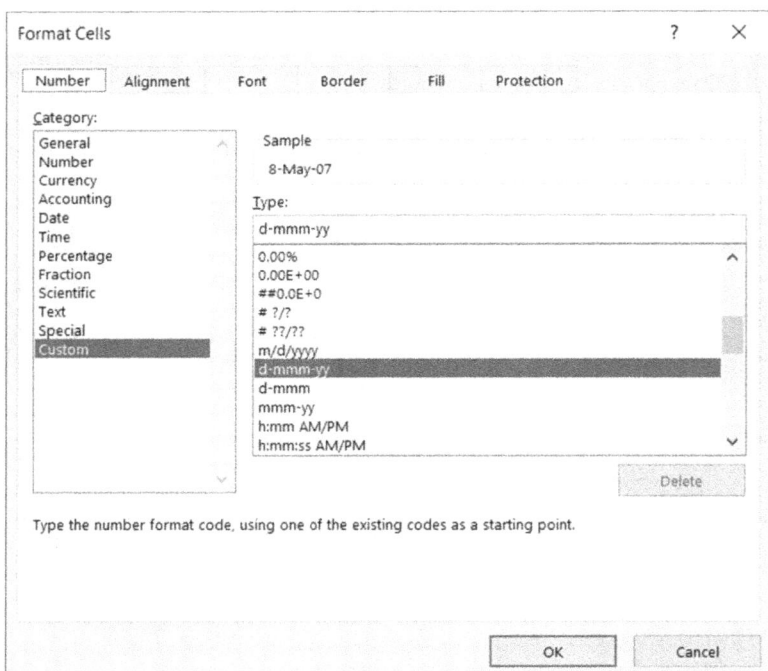

Format Cells ? ✕

Number | Alignment | Font | Border | Fill | Protection

Category:

General
Number
Currency
Accounting
Date
Time
Percentage
Fraction
Scientific
Text
Special
Custom

Sample

8-May-07

Type:

d-mmm-yy

0.00%
0.00E+00
##0.0E+0
?/?
??/??
m/d/yyyy
d-mmm-yy
d-mmm
mmm-yy
h:mm AM/PM
h:mm:ss AM/PM

Delete

Type the number format code, using one of the existing codes as a starting point.

OK | Cancel

Figure 4.4: Cell Format Settings

CPM & GANTT ANALYSIS

The critical path model is further examined in this chapter where we showcase how a critical path is identified and how tasks are considered to be on the critical path. The critical path analysis only looks at schedule risk and does not affect the cost risk of a project.

Manually Solving a Critical Path Model

Using the complex network path shown in Figure 5.1, we illustrate how the critical path is calculated in Figure 5.2 using an Excel model. The example shows 21 tasks, each with its own optimistic (minimum), expected (likely), and pessimistic (maximum) duration. The earliest finish time is the earliest start time plus the simulated duration, where the earliest start time is the previous task's earliest finish time. If there are complex loops in a task's predecessors, then the maximum duration is used. The model is then completed with the calculation of last start time, last finish time, and the slack between last start time and earliest start time. If the slack is zero, meaning there is no extra buffer time, then it is considered to be a task that is on the critical path. Figure 5.3 shows the exact specifications of the calculations, complete with the rows and column headers.

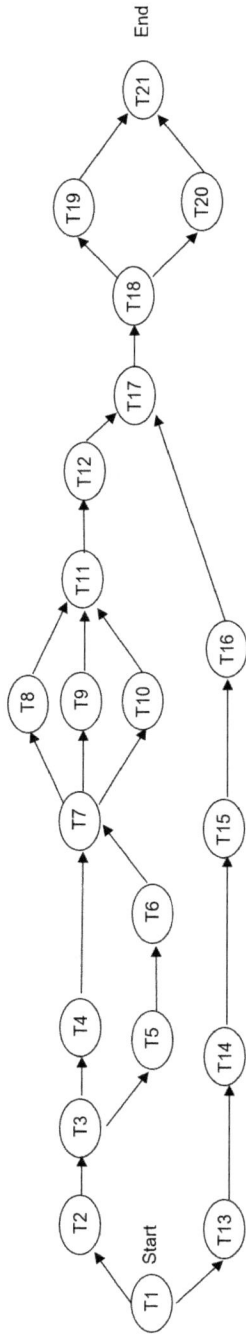

Figure 5.1: Critical Path Method (CPM)

Critical Path Method and Time to Market Analysis

Task Number	Predecessor	Duration Optimistic	Duration Expected	Duration Pessimistic	Simulated Duration	Earliest Start Time	Earliest Finish Time	Last Start Time	Last Finish Time	Slack	On Critical Path
Task 1		0	0	0	0.0	0.0	0.0	11.0	11.0	11.0	0
Task 2	1 FS	10	15	20	15.0	0.0	15.0	11.0	26.0	11.0	0
Task 3	2 FS	15	20	22	20.0	15.0	35.0	26.0	46.0	11.0	0
Task 4	3 FS	21	26	30	26.0	35.0	61.0	46.0	72.0	11.0	0
Task 5	3 SS	15	18	23	18.0	35.0	53.0	39.0	57.0	4.0	0
Task 6	5 FS	13	15	17	15.0	53.0	68.0	57.0	72.0	4.0	0
Task 7	4,6 FS	30	38	45	38.0	68.0	106.0	72.0	110.0	4.0	0
Task 8	7 FS	20	25	30	25.0	106.0	131.0	110.0	135.0	4.0	0
Task 9	7 FS	10	15	20	15.0	106.0	121.0	120.0	135.0	14.0	0
Task 10	7 FS	11	18	22	18.0	106.0	124.0	117.0	135.0	11.0	0
Task 11	8,9,10 FS	23	30	45	30.0	131.0	161.0	135.0	165.0	4.0	0
Task 12	11 FS	22	28	39	28.0	161.0	189.0	165.0	193.0	4.0	0
Task 13	1 FS	120	140	180	140.0	0.0	140.0	18.0	158.0	18.0	0
Task 14	13 FS	13	18	22	18.0	140.0	158.0	158.0	176.0	18.0	0
Task 15	14 SS	15	20	25	20.0	158.0	178.0	158.0	178.0	0.0	1
Task 16	15 FS	10	15	20	15.0	178.0	193.0	178.0	193.0	0.0	1
Task 17	12,16 FS	30	33	44	33.0	193.0	226.0	193.0	226.0	0.0	1
Task 18	17 FS	5	8	11	8.0	226.0	234.0	226.0	234.0	0.0	1
Task 19	18 FS	10	15	25	15.0	234.0	249.0	236.0	251.0	2.0	0
Task 20	18 FS	13	17	19	17.0	234.0	251.0	234.0	251.0	0.0	1
Task 21	19, 20 FS	20	25	40	25.0	251.0	276.0	251.0	276.0	0.0	1
End					0.0	276.0	276.0	276.0	276.0		

Figure 5.2: Critical Path Method (CPM)

Critical Path Method and Time to Market Analysis

	Task Number	Predecessor	Duration Optimistic	Duration Expected	Duration Pessimistic	Simulated Duration	Earliest Start Time	Earliest Finish Time	Last Start Time	Last Finish Time	Slack	On Critical Path
			D	E	F	G	H	I	J	K	L	M
4	Task 1		0	0	0	0	0	=H4+G4	=MIN(J5,J16)	=J4+G4		
5	Task 2	1 FS	10	15	20		=I4	=H5+G5	=J6-G5	=J5+G5	=J5-H5	=IF(L5=0,1,0)
6	Task 3	2 FS	15	20	22		=I5	=H6+G6	=MIN(J7-G6,J8)	=J6+G6	=J6-H6	=IF(L6=0,1,0)
7	Task 4	3 FS	21	26	30		=I6	=H7+G7	=J10-G7	=J7+G7	=J7-H7	=IF(L7=0,1,0)
8	Task 5	3 SS	15	18	23		=I6	=H8+G8	=J9-G8	=J8+G8	=J8-H8	=IF(L8=0,1,0)
9	Task 6	5 FS	13	15	17		=I8	=H9+G9	=J10-G9	=J9+G9	=J9-H9	=IF(L9=0,1,0)
10	Task 7	4,6 FS	30	38	45		=MAX(I7,I9)	=H10+G10	=MIN(J11-G10,J12-G10,J13)	=J10+G10	=J10-H10	=IF(L10=0,1,0)
11	Task 8	7 FS	20	25	30		=I10	=H11+G11	=J14-G11	=J11+G11	=J11-H11	=IF(L11=0,1,0)
12	Task 9	7 FS	10	15	20		=I10	=H12+G12	=J14-G12	=J12+G12	=J12-H12	=IF(L12=0,1,0)
13	Task 10	7 FS	11	18	22		=I10	=H13+G13	=J14-G13	=J13+G13	=J13-H13	=IF(L13=0,1,0)
14	Task 11	8,9,10 FS	23	30	45		=MAX(I11:I13)	=H14+G14	=J15-G14	=J14+G14	=J14-H14	=IF(L14=0,1,0)
15	Task 12	11 FS	22	28	39		=I14	=H15+G15	=J20-G15	=J15+G15	=J15-H15	=IF(L15=0,1,0)
16	Task 13	1 FS	120	140	180		=I4	=H16+G16	=J17-G16	=J16+G16	=J16-H16	=IF(L16=0,1,0)
17	Task 14	13 FS	13	18	22		=I16	=H17+G17	=J18	=J17+G17	=J17-H17	=IF(L17=0,1,0)
18	Task 15	14 SS	15	20	25		=I17	=H18+G18	=J19-G18	=J18+G18	=J18-H18	=IF(L18=0,1,0)
19	Task 16	15 FS	10	15	20		=I18	=H19+G19	=J20-G19	=J19+G19	=J19-H19	=IF(L19=0,1,0)
20	Task 17	12,16 FS	30	33	44		=MAX(I15,I19)	=H20+G20	=J21-G20	=J20+G20	=J20-H20	=IF(L20=0,1,0)
21	Task 18	17 FS	5	8	11		=I20	=H21+G21	=MIN(J22:J23)-G21	=J21+G21	=J21-H21	=IF(L21=0,1,0)
22	Task 19	18 FS	10	15	25		=I21	=H22+G22	=J24-G22	=J22+G22	=J22-H22	=IF(L22=0,1,0)
23	Task 20	18 FS	13	17	19		=I21	=H23+G23	=J24-G23	=J23+G23	=J23-H23	=IF(L23=0,1,0)
24	Task 21	19,20 FS	20	25	40		=MAX(I22:I23)	=H24+G24	=H24	=J24+G24	=J24-H24	=IF(L24=0,1,0)
25	End					0	=I24	=H25+G25	=H25	=J25+G25		

Figure 5.3: Manual Computations

Comparing with PEAT Calculations

Figure 5.4 is a replica of Figure 5.1's complex path using PEAT's project management module. The same input assumptions are entered in Figure 5.5. We see the single-point estimate's completion time of 276 days is the same as that calculated manually in Figure 5.2.

Notice that in Figure 5.2, the critical tasks were Tasks 15, 16, 17, 18, 20, and 21. In Figure 5.4, these same tasks are on the highlighted critical path. However, notice that by convention, a critical path is, by definition, a pathway, from the start of the project to the end of the project. Hence, Figure 5.4 shows the critical path from Task 1, 13, and 14 connecting to the critical tasks 15, 16, 17, 18, 20, and 21.

GANTT Charts

Figure 5.6 shows the development of a GANTT chart. GANTT charts are sometimes used in project management as a way of showing the tasks in rows displayed against time on the x-axis. On the left of the chart is a list of the tasks in rows and along the top is the time scale or dates.

The completed column is the earliest finish time of the preceding task multiplied by the percentage of completion (e.g., 4.5 is computed by $15 \times 30\%$) and the remaining is its complement value 10.5 or $15 \times (1-30\%)$. Finally, the start date column is the preceding task's date plus the simulated duration in Figure 5.2.

The GANTT chart is then generated based on these values that are shown as a horizontal bar chart with completed and remaining segments for each task.

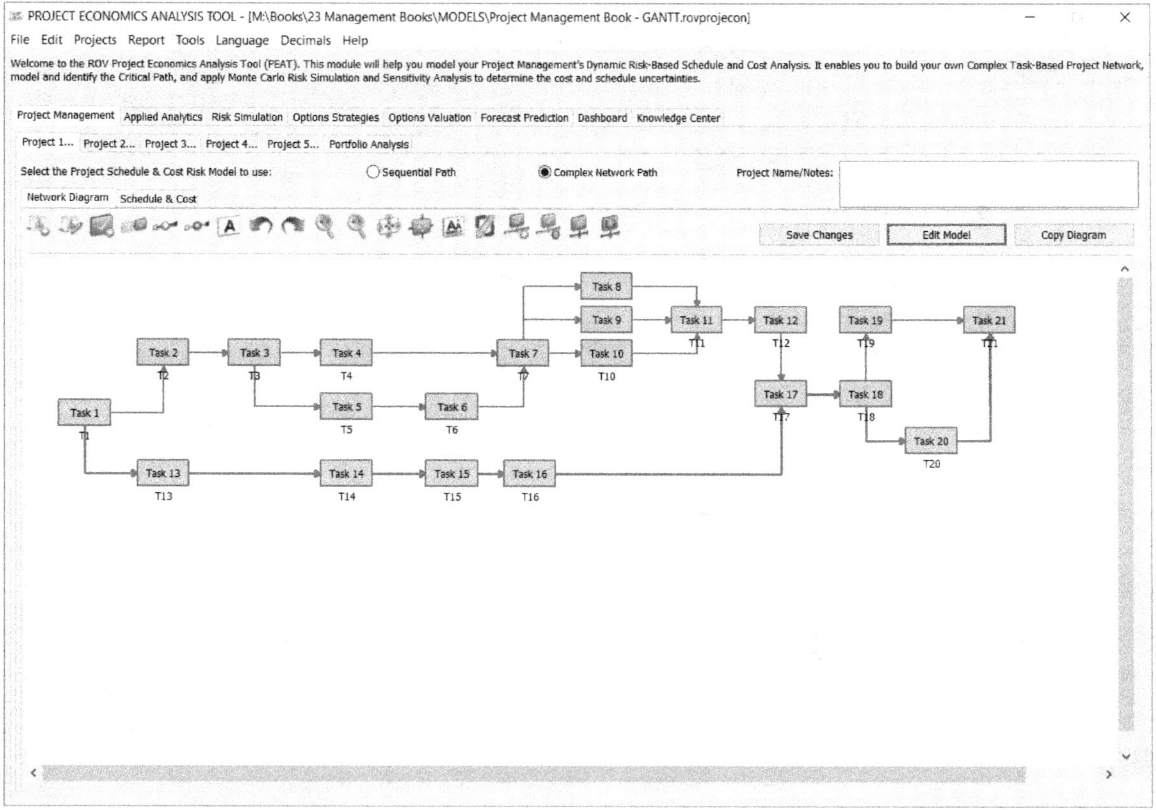

Figure 5.4: Complex Path in PEAT

File   Edit   Projects   Report   Tools   Language   Decimals   Help

Welcome to the ROV Project Economics Analysis Tool (PEAT). This module will help you model your Project Management's Dynamic Risk-Based Schedule and Cost Analysis. It enables you to build your own Complex Task-Based Project Network, model and identify the Critical Path, and apply Monte Carlo Risk Simulation and Sensitivity Analysis to determine the cost and schedule uncertainties.

Project Management | Applied Analytics   Risk Simulation   Options Strategies   Options Valuation   Forecast Prediction   Dashboard   Knowledge Center

Project 1...   Project 2...   Project 3...   Project 4...   Project 5...   Portfolio Analysis

Select the Project Schedule & Cost Risk Model to use: ○ Sequential Path   ● Complex Network Path

Project Name/Notes:

Network Diagram   Schedule & Cost

☑ Include Schedule-Based Cost Analysis   ☑ Perform Risk Simulation   Simulation Trials: 1,000   Run   Run All Projects
☐ Include Budget Overrun & Buffers   ☐ Apply Seed Value: 123   ☑ Auto Update   ☐ Run Sequentially
☐ Include Probabilities of Success of Each Task and Model Their Impacts   Show 21

		Tasks with	Weekly	Triangular
Task 7	T7	30	38	45
Task 8	T8	20	25	30
Task 9	T9	10	15	20
Task 10	T10	11	18	22
Task 11	T11	23	30	45
Task 12	T12	22	28	39
Task 13	T13	120	140	180
Task 14	T14	13	18	22
Task 15	T15	15	20	25
Task 16	T16	10	15	20
Task 17	T17	30	33	44
Task 18	T18	5	8	11
Task 19	T19	10	15	25
Task 20	T20	13	17	19
Task 21	T21	20	25	40

Project Total   226   276.00   361   0

Expected Total Duration
Critical Path 1, 13-19, 21   32.70%
Critical Path 1, 13-18, 20-21   29.10%
Critical Path 1-3, 5-8, 11-12, 17-19, 21   19.50%

Figure 5.5: Simulated Complex Path in PEAT

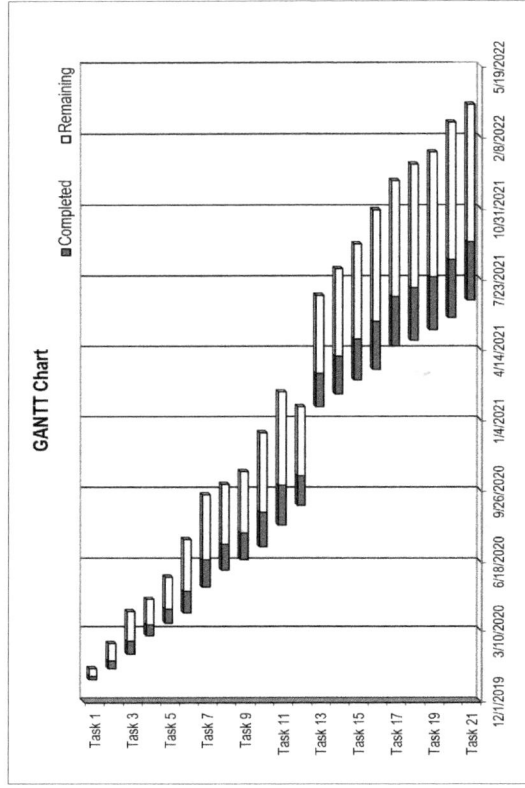

	Start Date	Completed	Remaining	%Complete	Date Value
Task 1	1/1/2020	4.5	10.5	30.00%	1/1/2020
Task 2	1/16/2020	10.5	24.5	30.00%	1/16/2020
Task 3	2/5/2020	18.3	42.7	30.00%	2/5/2020
Task 4	3/2/2020	15.9	37.1	30.00%	3/2/2020
Task 5	3/20/2020	20.4	47.6	30.00%	3/20/2020
Task 6	4/4/2020	31.8	74.2	30.00%	4/4/2020
Task 7	5/12/2020	39.3	91.7	30.00%	5/12/2020
Task 8	6/6/2020	36.3	84.7	30.00%	6/6/2020
Task 9	6/21/2020	37.2	86.8	30.00%	6/21/2020
Task 10	7/9/2020	48.3	112.7	30.00%	7/9/2020
Task 11	8/8/2020	56.7	132.3	30.00%	8/8/2020
Task 12	9/5/2020	42.0	98.0	30.00%	9/5/2020
Task 13	1/23/2021	47.4	110.6	30.00%	1/23/2021
Task 14	2/10/2021	53.4	124.6	30.00%	2/10/2021
Task 15	3/2/2021	57.9	135.1	30.00%	3/2/2021
Task 16	3/17/2021	67.8	158.2	30.00%	3/17/2021
Task 17	4/19/2021	70.2	163.8	30.00%	4/19/2021
Task 18	4/27/2021	74.7	174.3	30.00%	4/27/2021
Task 19	5/12/2021	75.3	175.7	30.00%	5/12/2021
Task 20	5/29/2021	82.8	193.2	30.00%	5/29/2021
Task 21	6/23/2021	82.8	193.2	30.00%	6/23/2021

Figure 5.6: GANTT Chart

OVERRUN BUFFERS & LINKED TASKS WITH PROBABILITY OF SUCCESS

Cost overruns and probabilities of success on each connected task can be included in the complex path model calculations. These inclusions will only affect a project's cost and not its schedule.

Basic Model, Cost Overruns, Probability of Success for Each Task

Figure 6.1 illustrates a basic sequential path model without any overrun assumptions or probabilities of success, while Figure 6.2 shows the same model with some overrun assumptions on the budget. Figure 6.3 uses probabilities of success on each task but without any budget overrun. Finally, Figure 6.4 shows the same model with both budget overruns and probabilities of success on each task. An identical simulation of 10,000 trials was run with a seed value of 123. This way, we can have a proper and direct comparison of these four models and see the effects of these overrun assumptions and probabilities of success on the schedule and cost risk profile.

File Edit Projects Report Tools Language Decimals Help

Welcome to the ROV Project Economics Analysis Tool (PEAT). This module will help you model your Project Management's Dynamic Risk-Based Schedule and Cost Analysis. It enables you to build your own Complex Task-Based Project Network, model and identify the Critical Path, and apply Monte Carlo Risk Simulation and Sensitivity Analysis to determine the cost and schedule uncertainties.

Project Management Applied Analytics Risk Simulation Options Strategies Options Valuation Forecast Prediction Dashboard Knowledge Center

Basic Overrun Probabilistic Complex Portfolio Analysis

Select the Project Schedule & Cost Risk Model to use:
Schedule & Cost   ● Sequential Path   ○ Complex Network Path   Project Name/Notes:

☑ Include Schedule-Based Cost Analysis   ☑ Perform Risk Simulation
☑ Include Budget Overrun & Buffers   ☑ Apply Seed Value: 123   Simulation Trials: 10,000   Run   Run All Projects
☑ Include Probabilities of Success of Each Task and Model Their Impacts   Show 14   Tasks with Weekly   ☑ Auto Update ☐ Run Sequentially Triangular

Task	Task Name	Cost (Fixed Cost)			Computed Cost	Time Schedule (Weeks)			Variable Weekly Cost	Overrun Assumption	Probability of Success	Linked Events
		Minimum	Most Likely	Maximum		Minimum	Most Likely	Maximum				
Task 1	Conceptualization	1,845	2,783	5,595	5,033	1	1.5	3	1,500			1
Task 2	Added time for remodeling product	158	908	1,845	1,658	0.1	0.5	1	1,500			1
Task 3	Initiation	6,220	9,345	15,595	16,845	2	3	5	2,500			1
Task 4	Reworking concept	908	1,845	3,720	3,345	0.5	1	2	1,500			1
Task 5	Modification of existing concepts	908	1,845	2,783	3,345	0.5	1	1.5	1,500			1
Task 6	Phase 2 Development	21,845	26,220	34,970	47,220	5	6	8	3,500			1
Task 7	Additional R&D	1,220	1,845	2,470	3,345	1	1.5	2	1,000			1
Task 8	Apply external IP	3,095	6,220	6,220	11,220	0.5	1	1	5,000			1
Task 9	Manufacturing	62,470	99,970	124,970	179,970	5	8	10	10,000			1
Task 10	Reprototyping	9,970	14,970	19,970	26,970	1	1.5	2	8,000			1
Task 11	Recasting and rework	9,970	14,970	19,970	26,970	1	1.5	2	8,000			1
Task 12	Market Analysis	149,970	187,470	299,970	337,470	4	5	8	30,000			1
Task 13	Additional market research	12,470	24,970	37,470	44,970	1	2	3	10,000			1
Task 14	Repositioning	24,970	37,470	62,470	67,470	2	3	5	10,000			1
	Project Total Cost	306,019	430,831	638,018	775,831	25	36.50	54	345,000			

Figure 6.1: Basic Model without Budget Overrun and Probability of Success

PROJECT ECONOMICS ANALYSIS TOOL - [M:\Books\23 Management Books\MODELS\Project Management Book - More Models\rovproject.con]

File   Edit   Projects   Report   Tools   Language   Decimals   Help

Welcome to the ROV Project Economics Analysis Tool (PEAT). This module will help you model your Project Management's Dynamic Risk-Based Schedule and Cost Analysis. It enables you to build your own Complex Task-Based Project Network, model and identify the Critical Path, and apply Monte Carlo Risk Simulation and Sensitivity Analysis to determine the cost and schedule uncertainties.

Project Management   Applied Analytics   Risk Simulation   Options Strategies   Options Valuation   Forecast Prediction   Dashboard   Knowledge Center

Basic   Overrun   Probabilistic   Complex   Portfolio Analysis

Select the Project Schedule & Cost Risk Model to use: ● Sequential Path   ○ Complex Network Path

Project Name/Notes:

Schedule & Cost

☑ Include Schedule-Based Cost Analysis   ☑ Perform Risk Simulation

☑ Include Budget Overrun & Buffers   ☑ Apply Seed Value: 123   Simulation Trials: 10,000   Run   Run All Projects

☑ Include Probabilities of Success of Each Task and Model Their Impacts   Show   14   Tasks with   Weekly   ☑ Auto Update   ☐ Run Sequentially

Triangular

Task	Task Name	Cost (Fixed Cost)			Computed Cost	Time Schedule (Weeks)			Variable Weekly Cost	Overrun Assumption	Probability of Success	Linked Events
		Minimum	Most Likely	Maximum		Minimum	Most Likely	Maximum				
Task 1	Conceptualization	1,845	2,783	5,595	5,536	1	1.5	3	1,500	10.00%		1
Task 2	Added time for remodeling product	158	908	1,845	1,824	0.1	0.5	1	1,500	10.00%		1
Task 3	Initiation	6,220	9,345	15,595	18,530	2	3	5	2,500	10.00%		1
Task 4	Reworking concept	908	1,845	3,720	3,345	0.5	1	2	1,500	0.00%		1
Task 5	Modification of existing concepts	908	1,845	2,783	3,345	0.5	1	1.5	1,500	0.00%		1
Task 6	Phase 2 Development	21,845	26,220	34,970	47,220	5	6	8	3,500	0.00%		1
Task 7	Additional R&D	1,220	1,845	2,470	3,345	1	1.5	2	1,000	0.00%		1
Task 8	Apply external IP	3,095	6,220	6,220	11,220	0.5	1	1	5,000	0.00%		1
Task 9	Manufacturing	62,470	99,970	124,970	179,970	5	8	10	10,000	0.00%		1
Task 10	Reprototyping	9,970	14,970	19,970	26,970	1	1.5	2	8,000	0.00%		1
Task 11	Recasting and rework	9,970	14,970	19,970	26,970	1	1.5	2	8,000	0.00%		1
Task 12	Market Analysis	149,970	187,470	299,970	371,217	4	5	8	30,000	10.00%		1
Task 13	Additional market research	12,470	24,970	37,470	49,467	1	2	3	10,000	10.00%		1
Task 14	Repositioning	24,970	37,470	62,470	74,217	2	3	5	10,000	10.00%		1
	Project Total Cost	**306,019**	**430,831**	**638,018**	**823,176**	**25**	**36.50**	**54**	**392,345**			

Figure 6.2: Budget Overrun

PROJECT ECONOMICS ANALYSIS TOOL - [M:\Books\23 Management Books\MODELS\Project Management Book - More Models.rovprojecon] — □ ×

File   Edit   Projects   Report   Tools   Language   Decimals   Help

Welcome to the ROV Project Economics Analysis Tool (PEAT). This module will help you model your Project Management's Dynamic Risk-Based Schedule and Cost Analysis. It enables you to build your own Complex Task-Based Project Network, model and identify the Critical Path, and apply Monte Carlo Risk Simulation and Sensitivity Analysis to determine the cost and schedule uncertainties.

Project Management   Applied Analytics   Risk Simulation   Options Strategies   Options Valuation   Forecast Prediction   Dashboard   Knowledge Center

Basic   Overrun   Probabilistic   Complex   Portfolio Analysis

Select the Project Schedule & Cost Risk Model to use: ● Sequential Path   ○ Complex Network Path   Project Name/Notes:

Schedule & Cost

☑ Include Schedule-Based Cost Analysis   ☑ Perform Risk Simulation
☑ Include Budget Overrun & Buffers   ☑ Apply Seed Value:
☑ Include Probabilities of Success of Each Task and Model Their Impacts

Simulation Trials: 123 / 10,000   Run   ☑ Auto Update   Run All Projects
Tasks with Weekly   Show 14   ☐ Run Sequentially   Triangular

Task	Task Name	Cost (Fixed Cost) Minimum	Most Likely	Maximum	Computed Cost	Time Schedule (Weeks) Minimum	Most Likely	Maximum	Variable Weekly Cost	Overrun Assumption	Probability of Success	Linked Events
Task 1	Conceptualization	1,845	2,783	5,595	5,033		1.5	3	1,500		99.00%	1
Task 2	Added time for remodeling product	158	908	1,845	1,658	0.1	0.5	1	1,500		95.00%	1
Task 3	Initiation	6,220	9,345	15,595	16,845	2	3	5	2,500		93.00%	1
Task 4	Reworking concept	908	1,845	3,720	3,345	0.5	1	2	1,500		99.00%	1
Task 5	Modification of existing concepts	908	1,845	2,783	3,345	0.5	1	1.5	1,500		99.00%	1
Task 6	Phase 2 Development	21,845	26,220	34,970	47,220	5	6	8	3,500		50.00%	1
Task 7	Additional R&D	1,220	1,845	2,470	3,345	1	1.5	2	1,000		97.00%	1
Task 8	Apply external IP	3,095	6,220	6,220	11,220	0.5	1	1	5,000		98.00%	1
Task 9	Manufacturing	62,470	99,970	124,970	179,970	5	8	10	10,000		95.00%	1
Task 10	Reprototyping	9,970	14,970	19,970	26,970	1	1.5	2	8,000		35.00%	1
Task 11	Recasting and rework	9,970	14,970	19,970	26,970	1	1.5	2	8,000		98.00%	1
Task 12	Market Analysis	149,970	187,470	299,970	337,470	4	5	8	30,000		90.00%	1
Task 13	Additional market research	12,470	24,970	37,470	44,970	1	2	3	10,000		95.00%	1
Task 14	Repositioning	24,970	37,470	62,470	67,470	2	3	5	10,000		95.00%	1
	Project Total Cost	306,019	430,831	638,018	775,831	25	36.50	54	345,000			

Figure 6.3: Probability of Success

PROJECT ECONOMICS ANALYSIS TOOL - [M:\Books\23 Management Books\MODELS\Project Management Book - More Models\rovprojecon] — □ ×

File Edit Projects Report Tools Language Decimals Help

Welcome to the ROV Project Economics Analysis Tool (PEAT). This module will help you model your Project Management's Dynamic Risk-Based Schedule and Cost Analysis. It enables you to build your own Complex Task-Based Project Network, model and identify the Critical Path, and apply Monte Carlo Risk Simulation and Sensitivity Analysis to determine the cost and schedule uncertainties.

Project Management Applied Analytics Risk Simulation Options Strategies Options Valuation Forecast Prediction Dashboard Knowledge Center

Basic Overrun Probabilistic Complex Portfolio Analysis

Select the Project Schedule & Cost Risk Model to use: ● Sequential Path   ○ Complex Network Path   Project Name/Notes:

Schedule & Cost
☑ Include Schedule-Based Cost Analysis   ☑ Perform Risk Simulation
☑ Include Budget Overrun & Buffers   ☑ Apply Seed Value:
☑ Include Probabilities of Success of Each Task and Model Their Impacts

Simulation Trials: 123   10,000
Tasks with: Weekly   14
Show

Run   Run All Projects
☑ Auto Update   ☐ Run Sequentially
Weekly   Triangular

Task	Task Name	Cost (Fixed Cost)			Computed Cost	Time Schedule (Weeks)			Variable Weekly Cost	Overrun Assumption	Probability of Success	Linked Events
		Minimum	Most Likely	Maximum		Minimum	Most Likely	Maximum				
Task 1	Conceptualization	1,845	2,783	5,595	5,536	1	1.5	3	1,500	10.00%	99.00%	1
Task 2	Added time for remodeling product	158	908	1,845	1,824	0.1	0.5	1	1,500	10.00%	95.00%	1
Task 3	Initiation	6,220	9,345	15,595	18,530	2	3	5	2,500	10.00%	93.00%	1
Task 4	Reworking concept	908	1,845	3,720	3,345	0.5	1	2	1,500	0.00%	99.00%	1
Task 5	Modification of existing concepts	908	1,845	2,783	3,345	0.5	1	1.5	1,500	0.00%	99.00%	1
Task 6	Phase 2 Development	21,845	26,220	34,970	47,220	5	6	8	3,500	0.00%	50.00%	1
Task 7	Additional R&D	1,220	1,845	2,470	3,345	1	1.5	2	1,000	0.00%	97.00%	1
Task 8	Apply external IP	3,095	6,220	6,220	11,220	0.5	1	1	5,000	0.00%	98.00%	1
Task 9	Manufacturing	62,470	99,970	124,970	179,970	5	8	10	10,000	0.00%	95.00%	1
Task 10	Reprototyping	9,970	14,970	19,970	26,970	1	1.5	2	8,000	0.00%	35.00%	1
Task 11	Recasting and rework	9,970	14,970	19,970	26,970	1	1.5	2	8,000	0.00%	98.00%	1
Task 12	Market Analysis	149,970	187,470	299,970	371,217	4	5	8	30,000	10.00%	90.00%	1
Task 13	Additional market research	12,470	24,970	37,470	49,467	1	2	3	10,000	10.00%	95.00%	1
Task 14	Repositioning	24,970	37,470	62,470	74,217	2	3	5	10,000	10.00%	95.00%	1
	Project Total Cost	306,019	430,831	638,018	823,176	25	36.50	54	392,345			

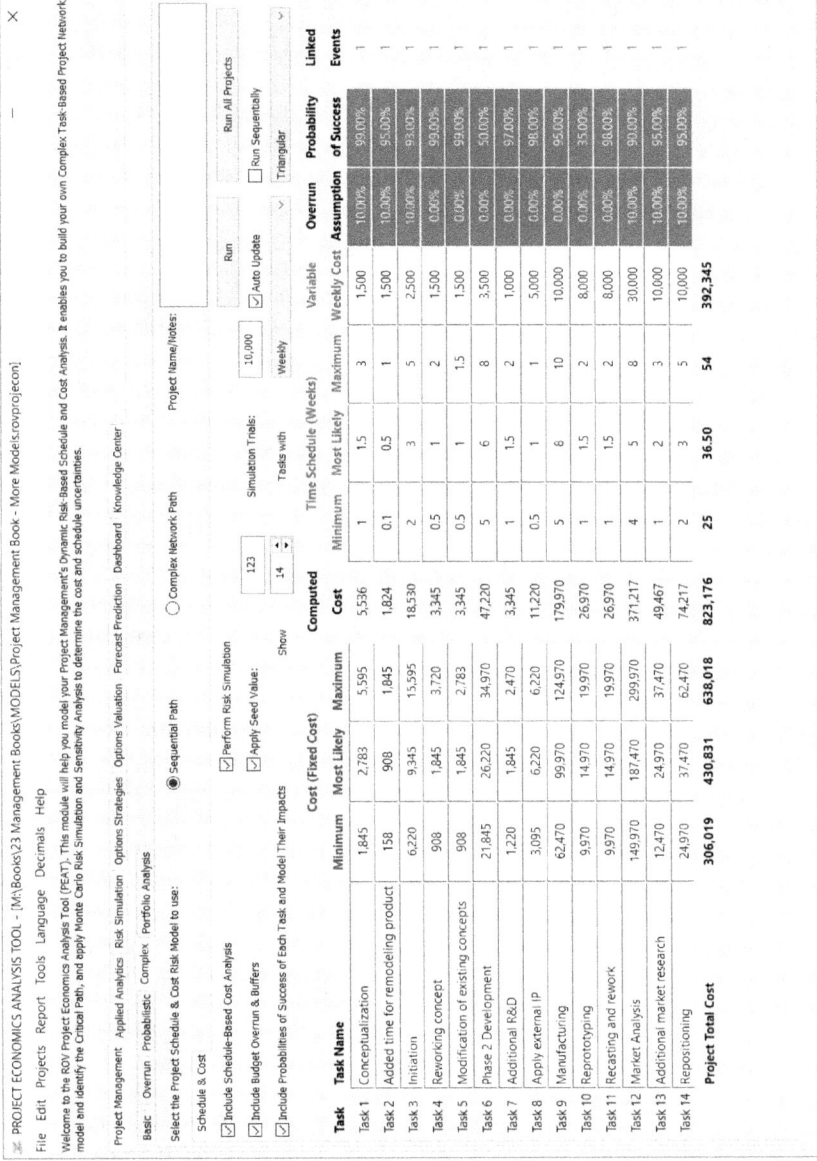

Figure 6.4: Budget Overrun and Probability of Success

Results Comparison

Figures 6.5, 6.6, and 6.7 show the results comparison for the four models described previously. Below are several key observations:

- Project Schedule is unchanged in all four models. Specifically, the *expected project schedules* are all identical (36.5 weeks). Further, the simulated probabilities on schedules are statistically identical (*simulated average project schedule* and the *90% percentile schedule*) and are only subjected to minor rounding differences (38.2 weeks and 40.6 weeks, respectively) caused by the random number generator of the simulation process.

- Single-point estimate values of expected project costs for the basic model and task probabilities model are identical ($775,831) because the probability is only applied when simulation is applied. Hence, single-point estimates would reveal identical values. Further, the budget overrun model and complex model with probabilities and overrun will yield identical expected project costs ($823,176) as they both include a budget overrun, which would, of course, generate higher costs than the basic model ($775,831).

- The simulated average project costs for probabilistic tasks and budget overrun (complex project) show a significantly reduced value ($191,705 and $198,606, respectively). This is because when a task fails, all subsequent tasks' costs are not incurred, and the project terminates. So, with a probabilistic task model, there is a chance the project will terminate at various points and the simulated average costs will show that. However, a 90th percentile of the costs will still yield a higher value but not as high as the models with nonprobabilistic tasks.

- Finally, Figure 6.7 shows that the costs are trimodal, with three potential stages of completion of the project. Figure 6.4's low probabilistic inputs (50%, 35%) delineate the tasks into three groups (Tasks 1–5, 6–9, and 10–14).

File   Edit   Projects   Report   Tools   Language   Decimals   Help

Welcome to the ROV Project Economics Analysis Tool (PEAT). This module will help you model your Project Management's Dynamic Risk-Based Schedule and Cost Analysis. It enables you to build your own Complex Task-Based Project Network, model and identify the Critical Path, and apply Monte Carlo Risk Simulation and Sensitivity Analysis to determine the cost and schedule uncertainties.

Project Management   Applied Analytics   Risk Simulation   Options Valuation   Forecast Prediction   Dashboard   Knowledge Center

Basic   Overrun   Probabilistic   Complex   Portfolio Analysis

Analysis of Alternatives (No Base Case)
○ Incremental Analysis (Choose Base Case):
Basic

☐ Run Sequentially

Run All Projects

90.00%

Economic Results	Basic	Overrun	Probabili...	Complex
Expected Project Cost	775,831	823,176	775,831	823,176
Expected Project Schedule	36.50	36.50	36.50	36.50
Simulated Average Project Cost	824,954	878,548	191,705	198,606
Simulated Average Project Schedule	38.18	38.20	38.22	38.21
Probability Expected Cost Will Overrun	85.51%	86.32%	9.58%	9.19%
Probability Expected Schedule Will Overrun	81.07%	80.76%	81.45%	81.16%
90.00% Percentile Cost	886,053	945,071	770,055	809,163
90.00% Percentile Schedule	40.64	40.63	40.67	40.64

Expected Project Cost   Probability Expected Cost Will Overrun   90.00% Percentile Cost

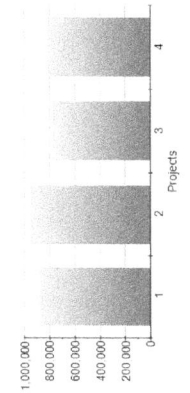

90.00% Percentile Cost   Investment Portfolio View   90.00% Percentile Cost

Charts...   Copy Chart   Charts...   2D Bar   Copy Chart

Both

Investment Portfolio View

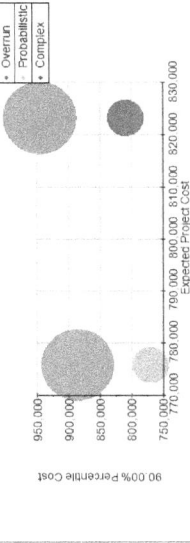

90.00% Percentile Cost

950 000
900 000
850 000
800 000

750 000 770 000 790 000 810 000 820 000 830 000
         760 000 780 000 800 000
         Expected Project Cost

● Basic
● Overrun
● Probabilistic
● Complex

Y axis

90.00% Percentile Cost

1 000 000
800 000
600 000
400 000
200 000
0
        1   2   3   4
            Projects

Figure 6.5: Comparative Analysis

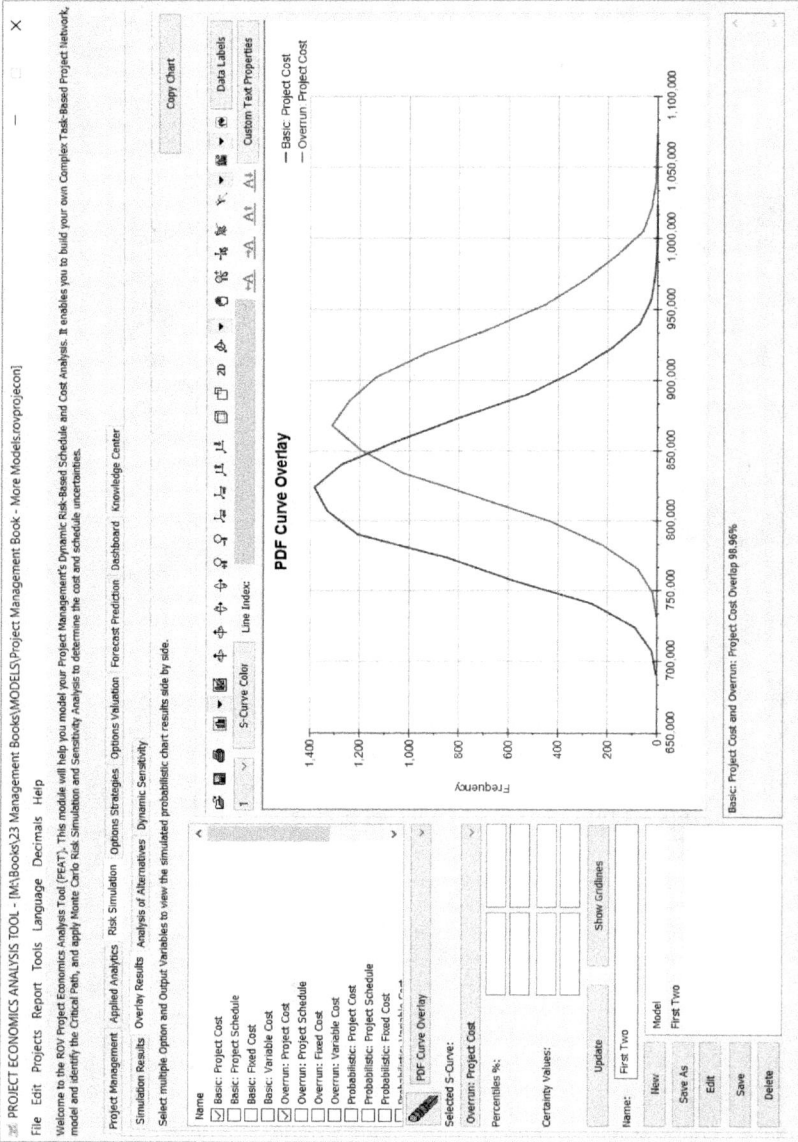

Figure 6.6: Overlay of Basic and Overrun Models

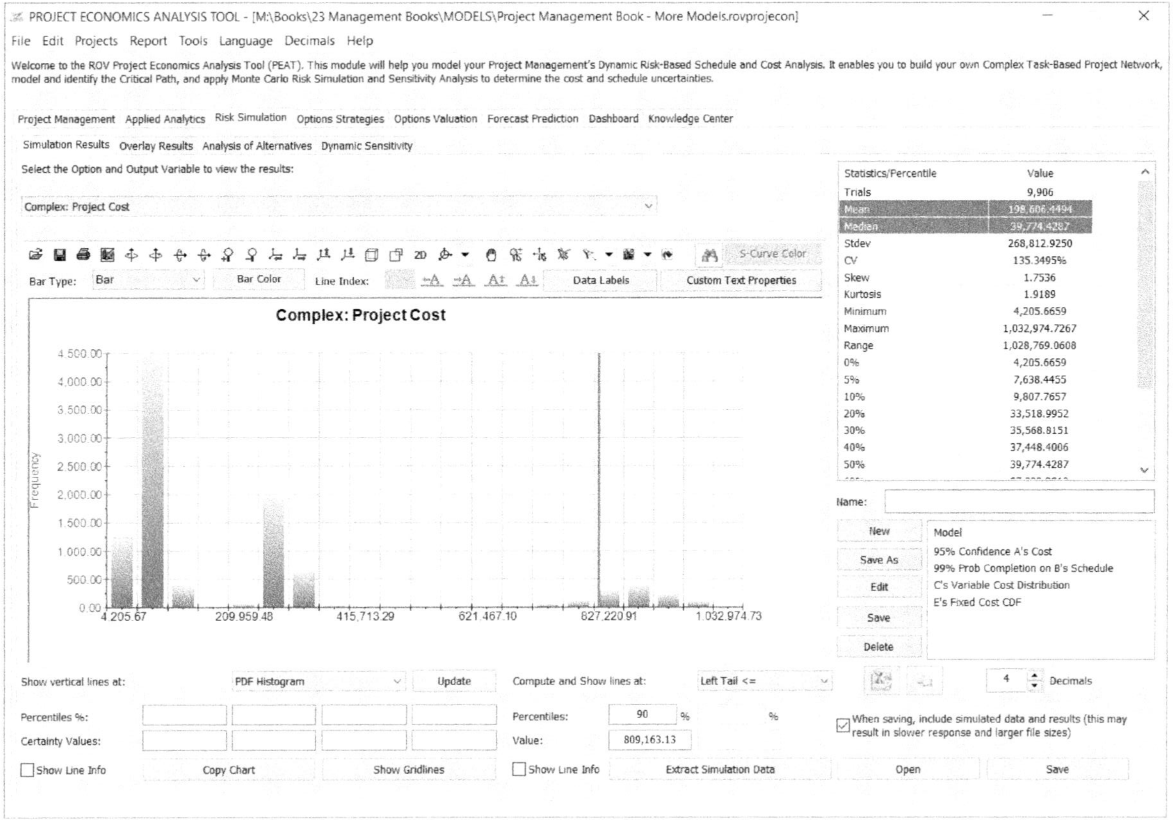

Figure 6.7: Trimodal Simulated Cost Structure

PROJECT ECONOMICS ANALYSIS TOOL - [M:\Books\23 Management Books\MODELS\Project Management Book - More Models\rovprojecon] — □ ×

File Edit Projects Report Tools Language Decimals Help

Welcome to the ROV Project Economics Analysis Tool (PEAT). This module will help you model your Project Management's Dynamic Risk-Based Schedule and Cost Analysis. It enables you to build your own Complex Task-Based Project Network, model and identify the Critical Path, and apply Monte Carlo Risk Simulation and Sensitivity Analysis to determine the cost and schedule uncertainties.

Project Management Applied Analytics Risk Simulation Options Strategies Options Valuation Forecast Prediction Dashboard Knowledge Center

Simulation Results Overlay Results Analysis of Alternatives Dynamic Sensitivity

You can compare the dynamic simulated results of all your options. A simulation must first be run before you can obtain any results. Choose if you wish to compare all options as standalone (Analysis of Alternatives) or against a base case (Incremental Analysis).

ANALYSIS OF ALTERNATIVES AND BASE CASE INCREMENTAL ANALYSIS

● Analysis of Alternatives (No Base Case)   ○ Incremental Analysis (Choose Base Case):

Economic Results: Project Cost

OPTIONS	Basic	Overrun	Probabilistic	Complex
Mean	824,904.06	878,547.90	191,704.94	198,676.45
Median	823,295.25	876,466.56	36,881.18	39,774.43
Stdev	45,668.16	50,044.23	255,187.72	268,812.92
Variance	2.09E+009	2.50E+009	6.51E+010	7.23E-010
CV	5.54%	5.70%	133.11%	135.35%
Skew	0.2107	0.1989	1.6680	1.7536
Kurtosis	-0.2287	-0.2515	1.6313	1.9189
Minimum	690,743.91	731,373.83	3,729.92	4,205.67
Maximum	1,022,978.35	1,073,266.53	952,636.53	1,032,974.73
Range	332,234.43	341,892.71	948,906.62	1,028,769.06
0% Percentile	690,743.91	731,373.83	3,729.92	4,205.67
5% Percentile	753,053.01	799,581.87	6,851.11	7,638.45
10% Percentile	766,583.63	815,371.46	8,612.31	9,807.77
20% Percentile	785,004.79	834,102.15	30,841.15	33,519.00
30% Percentile	798,551.49	850,087.61	32,972.26	35,568.82
40% Percentile	810,889.18	863,215.42	34,676.14	37,448.40
50% Percentile	823,295.25	876,466.56	36,881.18	39,774.43
60% Percentile	835,461.82	889,936.84	96,724.21	97,322.28
70% Percentile	848,625.79	904,651.48	262,466.22	264,918.65
80% Percentile	864,432.31	921,805.14	281,622.72	283,605.34
90% Percentile	886,052.74	945,071.43	770,055.43	809,163.13
95% Percentile	903,417.19	964,567.70	828,463.19	883,970.54
100% Percentile	1,022,978.35	1,073,266.53	952,636.53	1,032,974.73

Basic 2 ▲▼ Decimals

Project Cost (Options)

150.00 %

100.00 %

50.00 %

0.00 %

1   2   3   4

Options

2D Bar   Copy Chart

Figure 6.8: Expected Cost and Project Volatility

PRICING MODELS USING COST, RISK, & OPPORTUNITY

Sometimes, modeling tasks are used not for scheduling purposes but for costing purposes. For instance, in developing a government bid, a corporation may be required to submit a cost estimate and a bid based on the cost estimation model. Developing an incorrect cost estimate may result in losing the bid (overbidding with an incorrectly inflated cost) or obtaining the bid and losing money (under-costing and, hence, under-bidding on a firm fixed price project).

Work Breakout Structure Cost Models

Typically, in a cost and pricing model, we bypass a complex model because complex models are important in schedule estimation whereas cost estimations require the summation of all costs, regardless of whether a specific task lies on the critical path. Therefore, the typical cost pricing approach uses a work breakout structure (WBS) where the tasks are all assumed to run sequentially, and the risk spreads are used to set up the Monte Carlo risk simulation runs.

Cost + Risk – Opportunities

Typically, the WBS lists the tasks to be performed and these will constitute the costs of the program. Sometimes, risk elements as well as opportunities are added to the cost analysis. Specifically, risk elements are considered added costs (e.g., risk of rework or risk of raw material price increase), whereas upside opportunities are considered as a reduction in cost (i.e., a potential revenue stream). Hence, the total cost for the program is typically denoted as WBS Cost + Additional Risk – Upside Opportunities.

PEAT Cost Pricing Module

Figures 7.1–7.4 illustrate the use of PEAT's S-Curve Costing Model to run the WBS cost simulation for cost, risks, and opportunities. The following provides some additional information on how the model is set up and run in the software:

- *Input Assumptions.* This is where the Cost, Risk, Opportunity, and Risk Spreads are entered for the program.

- *Risk Simulation.* This is the heart of the tool where the risk simulation is performed and the resulting S-Curves are obtained, including all the ancillary statistics.

- *Return on Sales.* This module computes the various government bid contract types, such as Cost Plus Award Fee, Cost Plus Incentive Fee, Cost Plus Fixed Fee, Firm Fixed Price, Fixed Price Incentive Firm, and Fixed Price Incentive Successive Targets, and utilizes the results of risk simulated percentiles in its computations.

- *Range of Financial Outcomes.* This module takes the results from the Return on Sales (ROS) tab and provides a summary of the range of financial outcomes and returns the most critical pieces of information from the ROS model.

- *Knowledge Center.* This module includes a quick set of S-Curve Lessons (the basics of interpreting S-Curves), Getting Started Videos (quick lessons and introductions on using the tool), and Step by Step Procedures (this includes quick getting started steps in using the tool, that provide the analyst with a jump start instead of having to read lengthy user manuals).

In the software, click on *File | Load Example* to run a default example model with preconfigured settings and data (Figure 7.1). By default, the first tab shown is the *Input Assumptions* tab, showing the *Cost*, *Risk*, *Opportunity*, and *Spread Tables* subtabs with previously entered and saved data.

In the *Cost* subtab, some data already exists for you to get started. You can, in your own model, manually type in the data or copy and paste your data into the grid. Simply copy your data from another source (such as a text file, Word document, Excel file, etc.), select the cell or cells you wish to paste, and click on *Edit | Paste* or *right-click* and select *Paste*. Enter or paste your cost WBS Items and the Expected Value, and select the Risk Spread as appropriate for each WBS row.

Repeat the same steps above in the *Risk* and *Opportunity* subtabs. However, in those tabs, there is an extra column called Probability that requires input.

The data input portion of this tool is relatively straightforward but the following are some helpful tips to increase your productivity in using the tool:

- Columns that are inputs are colored *white*, whereas computed cells/columns are a light gray color. Also, not being able to click on a cell and type in a value indicates that that cell or column is a calculated output (e.g., Computed *Low/High* columns).

- Selecting the Spread from the drop-down list will automatically compute the *Computed High/Low* columns based on the spread level and distribution type selected. The Spreads are based on the Spread Tables subtab, which we will explore in a moment.

- The *Expected Value* column is user input and comprises static input values, whereas the Simulation column would be the computed/simulated results. When we run a risk simulation in the next few steps, you will see the values in this column dynamically change.

- The default is to show 100 rows, but you can change the number of rows to view as required. The same goes for the number of decimals to show (default is 0 decimals, where values are rounded to the nearest dollar). Please make sure you have enough rows before pasting data, otherwise there might be some missing data rows, or after pasting data, do not reduce the number of rows to less than the rows of data you have (of course, you will get a warning message if this happens) as some data might be accidentally deleted.

- You can also *Reset All Spreads* at once using the drop-down list on the top right of the user interface. This will reset all the Spreads for the subtab.

- *File | Data Encryption* and *Decryption* allows you to protect your data.

- Pasting data will only work on the *white* input cells. You cannot paste data on computed cells or a droplist like Risk Spreads.

- *Edit | Edit Spreads Droplist* allows you to configure which risk spreads are available in which of the Cost, Risk, or Opportunity subtabs.

- The headers can be clicked to sort the data. However, to facilitate sorting the dataset without empty rows, the tool will automatically reduce the number of visible rows to match the number of available rows of data before performing the sort. By sorting, you can look at WBS line items grouped by risk spreads or arranged in terms of expected value, and so forth.

- The *Spread* droplist can be copy and pasted. That is, you can select a spread for a specific line item, right-click *Copy* and then select multiple other rows and right-click *Paste* the same risk spread. This comes in handy when the WBS structure is large.

In the Spread Tables subtab (Figure 7.4) in the Input Assumptions tab is where the default risk spreads are entered. Continuing with the same example, click on the *Spread Tables* subtab in the main *Input Assumptions* tab.

The *Triangular* subtab shows the default *Symmetrical, Left Skew, and Right Skew* distributions for a Triangular distribution, and the 7 risk levels of each distribution skew-type. You can override these Low and High risk spread values but remember to click on *File | Save* to retain the changes or click on the *Restore Default Spreads* button to restore the default values if you make a mistake.

The following are some important notes to keep in mind when it comes to the risk spread tables:

- The Normal subtab shows the normal distribution's risk spread levels, just like the Triangular subtab, where you can change the spreads as required or keep the default values.

- In contrast, the *Program Specific*, or *Custom*, subtab allows you to enter your own *Risk Level Names* and *Risk Level Spreads* specific for the program under evaluation, up to 20 risk levels.

- When you edit or enter *Custom Spreads*, it *Auto-Saves* without prompting. When you re-open the software tool the next time, the entered custom spreads will be present.

- You can edit/change the default spreads by going to the installation path folder and editing the *Default Spreads.xml* file directly. You can edit this file in Notepad or Word, but please take care when doing so, as the current default spreads are based on the Air Force Cost Analysis Manual guidelines. The spreads in the tool cannot be edited directly to prevent any user errors.

- There is a *New Subcategory* available under the customized categories. This *New Subcategory* just creates an empty row devoid of any numerical inputs; whatever you put on this line is not used or calculated, but only used as a visual separation, such as if the user wants to say the following section is Level 3 rollup or Level 2 rollup of the WBS or a separate group of data/category within a WBS. This is not available by default but can be turned on easily. Simply go to *Edit | Edit Spread List* and check the *New Subcategory* selection at the bottom.

- If *No Selection* is made for a risk spread (i.e., either by not selecting something or selecting the blank line) this line item is taken out of the computation mix completely. In other words, no selection is like a placeholder for the user to temporarily put a line item in, but the inputs are not used in the calculations... this provides the user with some flexibility! Compare this to the drop-list selection of *No Risk* that means this line item is not simulated but the single-point expected value input is still used in the calculations.

This S-Curve tool allows you to enter in Costs, Risks and Opportunities, as well as their respective expected values and risk spreads, and run a Monte Carlo risk simulation based on the selected distributional skew and risk spread. The results will be presented as S-Curves (cumulative distribution function) and histograms (probability density functions).

Input Assumptions   Risk Simulation   Return on Sales (ROS)   Range of Financial Outcomes   Knowledge Center

Cost   Risk   Opportunity   Spread Tables

Enter the Cost, Risk, and Opportunity item names, their respective expected values, and the desired risk spread. The risk spreads will be automatically computed and Monte Carlo Risk Simulation will be applied on the computed distributions.

Grid: 500 Rows   Reset All Spreads with:
Show: 0 Decimals

N	ID	Item Name	Impact ($)	Spread	Computed Low	Computed High	Simulation
TOTAL			$320,000		$223,379	$610,354	
1	1	Automated Information System (AIS) Developed		NEW SUBCATEGORY			
2	1.1	Automated Information System Prime Mission Product Release/Increment 1..n (Specify)		NEW SUBCATEGORY			
3	1.1.1	Custom Application 1..n (Specify)		NEW SUBCATEGORY			
4	1.1.1.1	Custom Application 1..n (Specify) Subsystem Hardware 1..n (Specify)		NEW SUBCATEGORY			
5	1.1.1...	Custom Application 1..n (Specify) Subsystem Hardware 1..n (Specify) Hardware Product Engineering	$50,000	Triangular (Right Skew): Very High	$22,465	$132,665	
6	1.1.1...	Custom Application 1..n (Specify) Subsystem Hardware 1..n (Specify) Hardware Configuration Item (HWCI) 1..n (Specify)		NEW SUBCATEGORY			
7	1.1.1...	Custom Application 1..n (Specify) Subsystem Hardware 1..n (Specify) HWCI 1..n (Specify) Hardware Requirements	$10,000	Triangular (Right Skew): Low	$8,170	$15,515	
8	1.1.1...	Custom Application 1..n (Specify) Subsystem Hardware 1..n (Specify) HWCI 1..n (Specify) Hardware Architecture and Design	$10,000	Triangular (Right Skew): Average	$7,554	$17,353	
9	1.1.1...	Custom Application 1..n (Specify) Subsystem Hardware 1..n (Specify) HWCI 1..n (Specify) HW Prototyping	$10,000	Triangular (Right Skew): Medium	$6,938	$19,190	
10	1.1.1...	Custom Application 1..n (Specify) Subsystem Hardware 1..n (Specify) HWCI 1..n (Specify) COTS/GOTS HW Component Identification	$10,000	Triangular (Right Skew): Above Average	$6,322	$21,027	
11	1.1.1...	Custom Application 1..n (Specify) Subsystem Hardware 1..n (Specify) HWCI 1..n (Specify)	$10,000	Triangular (Right Skew): High	$5,705	$22,864	

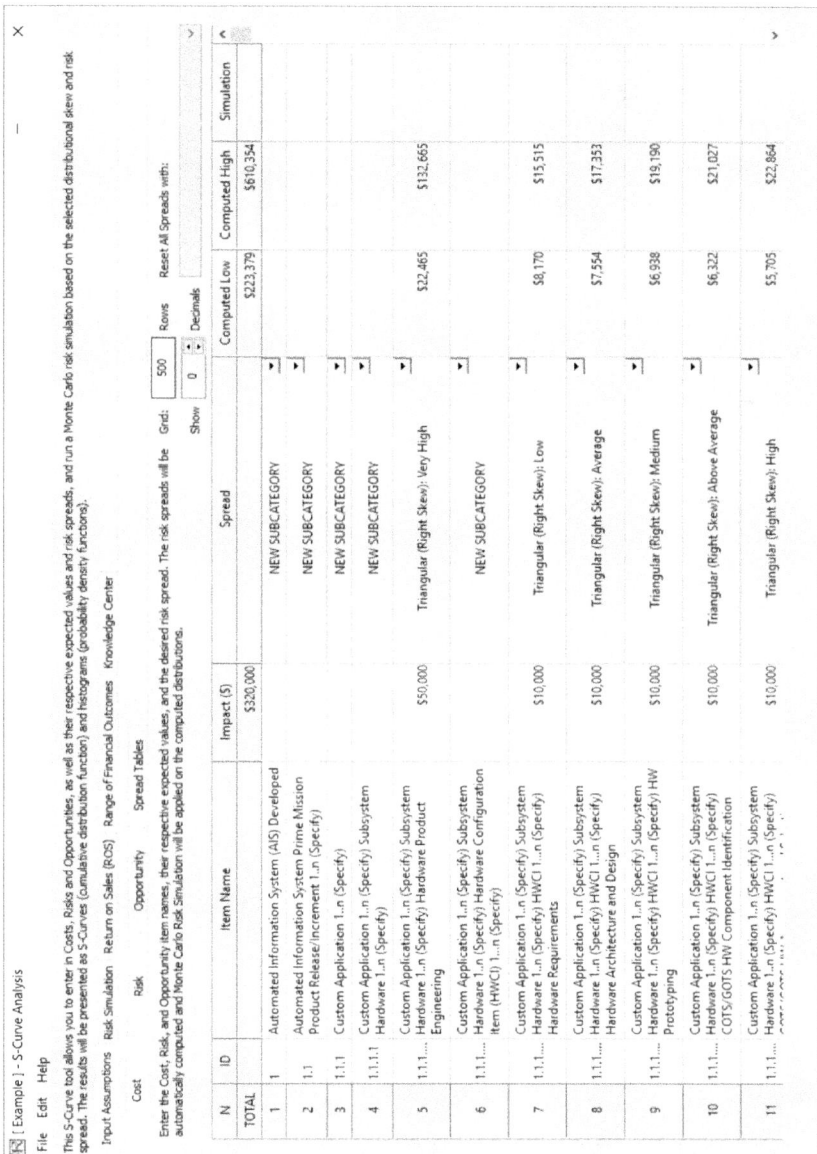

Figure 7.1: S-Curve Cost Pricing Software's Work Breakout Structure Costs

Input Assumptions   Risk Simulation   Return on Sales (ROS)   Range of Financial Outcomes   Knowledge Center

Cost   Risk   Opportunity   Spread Tables

Enter the Cost, Risk, and Opportunity item names, their respective expected values, and the desired risk spread. The risk spreads will be automatically computed and Monte Carlo Risk Simulation will be applied on the computed distributions.

Grid: 500 Rows   Show 0 Decimals

N	ID	Item Name	Impact ($)	Spread	Computed L	Reset All Spreads with:
TOTAL			$320,000		$22	Triangular (Symmetrical): Very High
						Triangular (Symmetrical): High
1	1	Automated Information System (AIS) Developed		NEW SUBCATEGORY		Triangular (Symmetrical): Above Average
						Triangular (Symmetrical): Medium
2	1.1	Automated Information System Prime Mission Product Release/Increment 1...n (Specify)		NEW SUBCATEGORY		Triangular (Symmetrical): Low
						Triangular (Symmetrical): Very Low
3	1.1.1	Custom Application 1...n (Specify)		NEW SUBCATEGORY		Triangular (Left Skew): Very High
						Triangular (Left Skew): High
4	1.1.1.1	Custom Application 1...n (Specify) Subsystem Hardware 1...n (Specify)		NEW SUBCATEGORY		Triangular (Left Skew): Above Average
						Triangular (Left Skew): Medium
						Triangular (Left Skew): Average
						Triangular (Left Skew): Low
5	1.1.1.....	Custom Application 1...n (Specify) Hardware Product Engineering	$50,000	Triangular (Right Skew): Very High	$2	Triangular (Left Skew): Very Low
						Triangular (Right Skew): Very High
						Triangular (Right Skew): High
6	1.1.1.....	Custom Application 1...n (Specify) Subsystem Hardware 1...n (Specify) Hardware Configuration Item (HWCI) 1...n (Specify)		NEW SUBCATEGORY		Triangular (Right Skew): Above Average
						Triangular (Right Skew): Medium
						Triangular (Right Skew): Average
						Triangular (Right Skew): Low
		Custom Application 1...n (Specify) Subsystem				Triangular (Right Skew): Very Low
						NO RISK

Figure 7.2: Simulation Assumption Spreads

This S-Curve tool allows you to enter in Costs, Risks and Opportunities, as well as their respective expected values and risk spreads, and run a Monte Carlo risk simulation based on the selected distributional skew and risk spread. The results will be presented as S-Curves (cumulative distribution function) and histograms (probability density functions).

Input Assumptions   Risk Simulation   Return on Sales (ROS)   Range of Financial Outcomes   Knowledge Center

| Cost | Risk | Opportunity | Spread Tables |

Enter the Cost, Risk, and Opportunity item names, their respective expected values, and the desired risk spread. The risk spreads will be automatically computed and Monte Carlo Risk Simulation will be applied on the computed distributions.

Grid: 500   Rows   Reset All Spreads with:

Show   0   Decimals

N	ID	Item Name	Impact ($)	Spread	PROB	Mean	Stdev	Simulation
TOTAL			$50,000			$34,689	$95,949	
1	R1	Risk 1 Title or Short Description	$10,000	Triangular (Right Skew): Low	50%	$8,170	$15,515	
2	R2	Risk 2 Title or Short Description	$10,000	Triangular (Right Skew): Average	60%	$7,554	$17,353	
3	R3	Risk 3 Title or Short Description	$10,000	Triangular (Right Skew): Medium	70%	$6,938	$19,190	
4	R4	Risk 4 Title or Short Description	$10,000	Triangular (Right Skew): Above Average	80%	$6,322	$21,027	
5	R5	Risk 5 Title or Short Description	$10,000	Triangular (Right Skew): High	90%	$5,705	$22,864	
6								
7								
8								
9								
10								
11								
12								
13								
14								
15								
16								
17								
18								
19								
20								
21								

Figure 7.3: Risks

File Edit Help

This S-Curve tool allows you to enter in Costs, Risks and Opportunities, as well as their respective expected values and risk spreads, and run a Monte Carlo risk simulation based on the selected distributional skew and risk spread. The results will be presented as S-Curves (cumulative distribution function) and histograms (probability density functions).

Input Assumptions Risk Simulation Return on Sales (ROS) Range of Financial Outcomes Knowledge Center

Cost   Risk   Opportunity   Spread Tables

The default risk spread settings are provided below. You can enter your own spreads if required but we recommend using the default spreads.

Reload Default Spreads

N	Triangular			Normal			Program Specific (Custom)		
	Symmetrical	Low	High	Left Skew	Low	High	Right Skew	Low	High
1	Very High	0.0000	2.1018	Very High	0.0000	1.5319	Very High	0.4493	2.6533
2	High	0.1421	1.8579	High	0.0000	1.4227	High	0.5705	2.2864
3	Above Average	0.2648	1.7352	Above Average	0.0000	1.3645	Above Average	0.6322	2.1027
4	Medium	0.3875	1.6125	Medium	0.0810	1.3062	Medium	0.6938	1.9190
5	Average	0.5103	1.4898	Average	0.2648	1.2446	Average	0.7554	1.7353
6	Low	0.6330	1.3670	Low	0.4485	1.1830	Low	0.8170	1.5515
7	Very Low	0.7558	1.2443	Very Low	0.6323	1.1214	Very Low	0.8786	1.3678

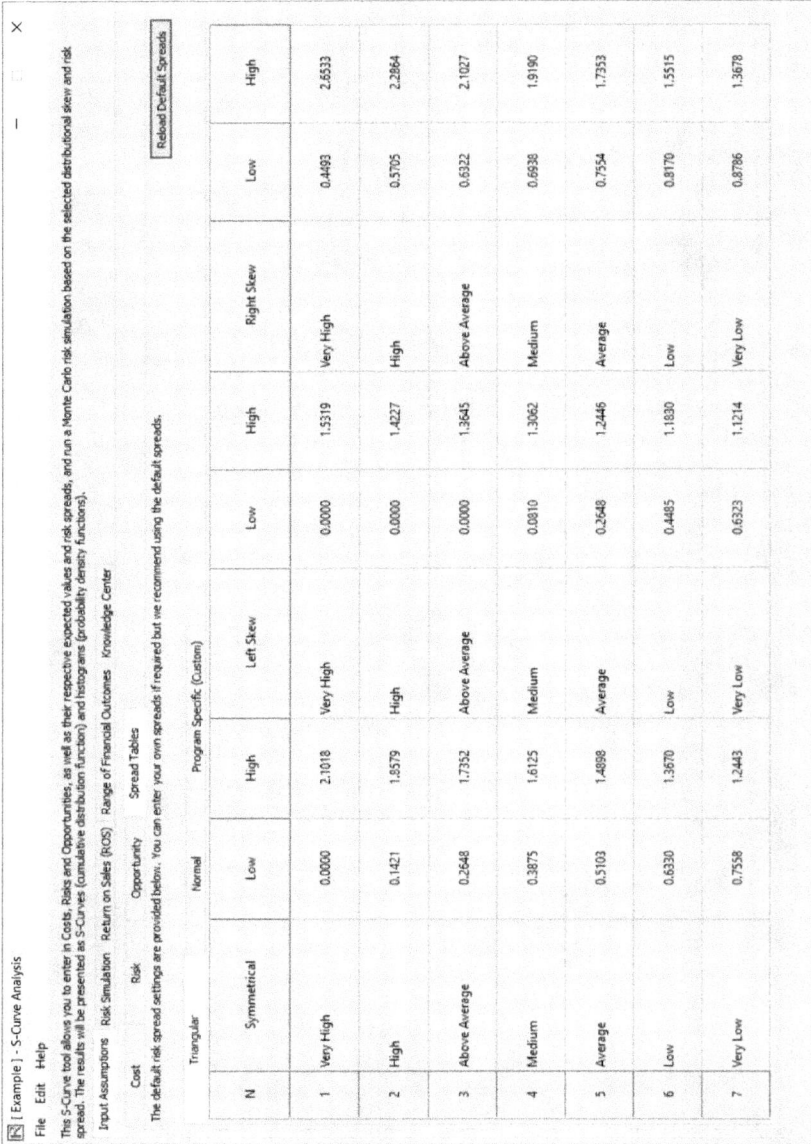

Figure 7.4: Simulation Spread Tables

Results Interpretation

Figure 7.5 shows the results from a Monte Carlo risk simulation. The CDF or cumulative distribution function is shown as a typical S-curve shape. Depending on the decision maker, the typical level to use in a bid is 75th to 85th percentile. In the current example, the 80th percentile is a bid price of $433,665. This result would not be possible and cannot be obtained without running a simulation. For example, single-point estimates would yield a total of $223,379 when summing all the minimum values and $610,354 if all maximum values are added together in the WBS.

[Example] - S-Curve Analysis

File   Edit   Help

This S-Curve tool allows you to enter in Costs, Risks and Opportunities, as well as their respective expected values and risk spreads, and run a Monte Carlo risk simulation based on the selected distributional skew and risk spread. The results will be presented as S-Curves (cumulative distribution function) and histograms (probability density functions).

Input Assumptions   Risk Simulation   Return on Sales (ROS)   Range of Financial Outcomes   Knowledge Center

Run the simulation and review the S-Curve results in the tabs. We recommend using the default settings for simplicity but you can always modify the settings and try out the various S-Curve settings.

Simulation Trials 10000

☑ Seed Value (Optional) 123   [Run Simulation]

Total GRO   Total Cost   Total Risk   Total Opportunity   Overlay

Bar Type: Bar | Bar Color | Line Index: 1 [20%] | Data Labels... | S-Curve Color | Custom Text Properties

Percentile	Value
0%	271,227
5%	374,232
10%	381,540
20%	389,823
30%	396,734
40%	402,717
50%	409,106
60%	416,436
70%	424,121
80%	433,666
90%	446,913
95%	457,504
100%	609,730

Statistics	Value
Trials	10,000
Mean	411,834
Median	409,106
Stdev	26,914
Variance	724,383,349
CV	6.54%
Skew	0.4362
Kurtosis	1.8330
Minimum	271,227
Maximum	609,730
Range	338,502

Copy Results | 0 ◆▶ Decimals

Open Simulation Results

Save Simulation Results

Show Gridlines | Extract Simulation Data | Create S-Curve in Excel

Copy Chart

Cumulative Probability

100%
90%
80%
70%
60%
50%
40%
30%
20%
10%
0%
271227   321227   371227   421227   471227   521227   571227   621227

20% 389,823
50% 409,106
80% 433,666 (BID)

S-Curve
Percentiles %:   20.00   50.00   80.00 | Update   80.00
Certainty Values:

Two Tails
Percentiles: %
Confidence: 80   %   433,665.62

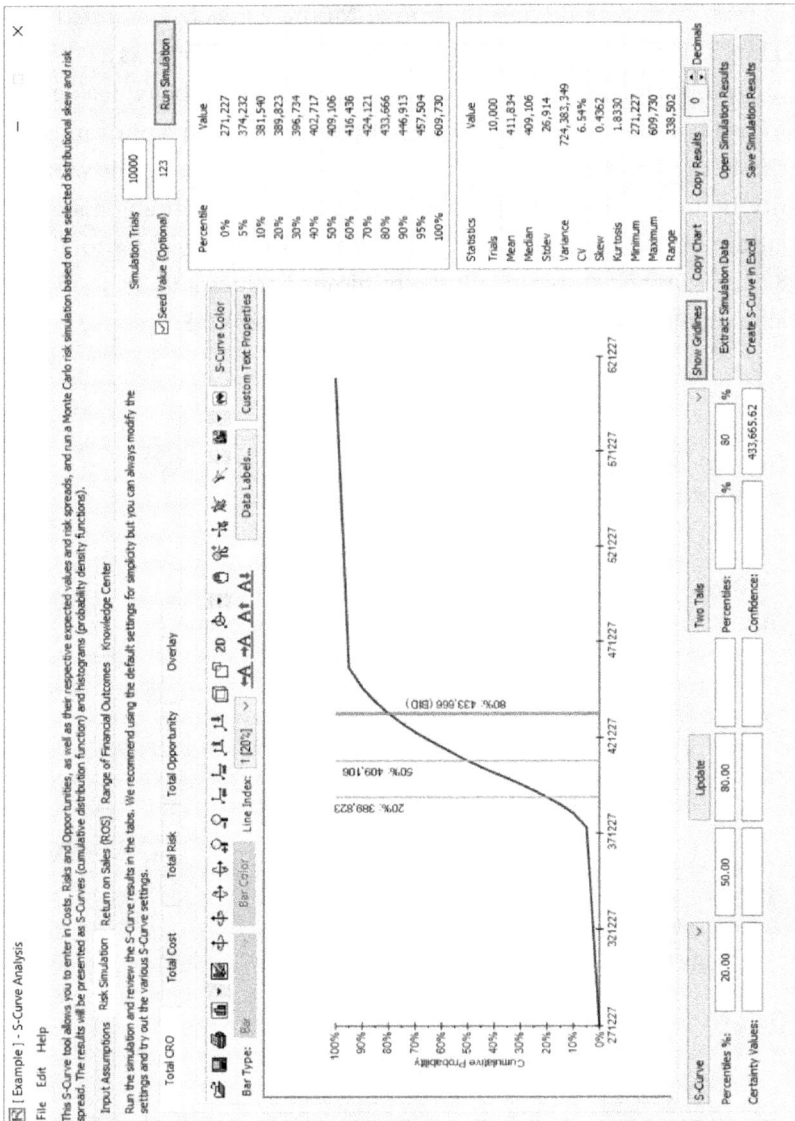

Figure 7.5: Simulated Cost Pricing S-Curve

[Example] - S-Curve Analysis

File   Edit   Help

This S-Curve tool allows you to enter in Costs, Risks and Opportunities, as well as their respective expected values and risk spreads, and run a Monte Carlo risk simulation based on the selected distributional skew and risk spread. The results will be presented as S-Curves (cumulative distribution function) and histograms (probability density functions).

Input Assumptions   Risk Simulation   Return on Sales (ROS)   Range of Financial Outcomes   Knowledge Center

STEP 1: Select the S-Curve:
- ☑ Cost + Risk - Opportunity
- ○ Cost   ○ Risk   ○ Custom

STEP 2: Select the Contract Type
- ○ Cost Plus Award Fee
- ○ Cost Plus Incentive Fee
- ○ Cost Plus Fixed Fee
- ☑ Firm Fixed Price
- ○ Fixed Price Incentive Firm

STEP 4: Compute   2 ⌄ Decimals
☐ Compute and Show All Models in ROFO

Compute   Copy   View All

STEP 3: Enter the following information by
☑ Divide S-Curve Percentiles by   1

Bid Cost/Target Cost	$434,131.86	
Award Fee (%)		
Fixed Fee (%)		
Profit (%)	15.00%	
MIN Target Cost Profit (%)		
Target Cost Profit (%)		
MAX Target Cost Profit (%)		
Buyer Share Ratio Underrun		
Buyer Share Ratio Overrun		
Ceiling Price (% of Target Cost)		

Northrop Grumman ROS Thresholds

	COST	COST + RISK	COST + RISK - OPP	CUSTOM
0%	251,402.30	290,737.54	271,227.45	
10%	354,348.34	396,832.26	381,539.96	
20%	362,598.88	405,002.19	389,823.25	
30%	369,200.13	411,674.68	396,734.09	
40%	374,910.63	417,738.79	402,717.37	
50%	381,335.23	423,997.75	409,105.84	
60%	388,464.49	431,316.11	416,436.18	
70%	396,265.34	439,055.96	424,120.80	
80%	405,873.54	448,499.55	433,665.62	
90%	418,753.05	461,575.80	446,912.59	
100%	568,598.50	632,820.95	609,729.68	

Share Ratio

	Buyer	Seller	Bid:										
			Target	Percentile	Profit	Price						
			$434,131.86	80.35%								

Underrun
Overrun

	0%	10%	20%	30%	40%	50%	60%	70%	80%	90%	100%	PTA	Ceiling
Profit													
Percentiles:	$271,227.45	$381,539.96	$389,823.25	$396,734.09	$402,717.37	$409,105.84	$416,436.18	$424,120.80	$433,665.62	$446,912.59	$609,729.68		
Target Cost	$434,131.86	$434,131.86	$434,131.86	$434,131.86	$434,131.86	$409,105.84	$434,131.86	$434,131.86	$433,665.62	$434,131.86	$434,131.86	Same	Same
Final Cost	$271,227.45	$381,539.96	$389,823.25	$396,734.09	$402,717.37	$409,105.84	$416,436.18	$424,120.80	$433,665.62	$446,912.59	$609,729.68	Same	Same
	Underrun	Underrun	Underrun	Underrun	Underrun	Underrun	Underrun	Underrun	Underrun	Overrun	Overrun		
Cost Delta (Final - Target)	$162,904.41	$52,591.90	$44,308.61	$37,397.77	$31,414.49	$25,026.02	$17,695.68	$10,011.06	$466.24	-$12,780.73	-$175,597...		

Figure 7.6: CRO Analysis Based on Contract Types

BUILDING A NEW HOUSE

This chapter showcases a project management example of building a new house. Instead of using the generic Task 1, Task 2, and so forth, as in previous chapters, this home-building example provides a more hands-on illustration of the PM module in PEAT, now that you are familiar with its algorithms and functionalities.

The example that follows assumes that a couple has decided to build their new dream home in northern California. The 0.5-acre land they are planning on purchasing costs $800,000. This is pending final negotiations and contract. Meanwhile, the couple is working with a general contractor to develop a plan to build their new home.

Steps in Building a New Home

After several consultations with the general contractor, the following tasks were developed in their project plan. The items with an * are to be run in parallel.

- Task 1: Land Purchase
- Task 2: Architectural Plans
- Task 3: Financing*
- Task 4: Permit*
- Task 5: Initial Walkthrough Orientation
- Task 6: Excavation
- Task 7: Footings*

- Task 8: Foundation*
- Task 9: Drainage*
- Task 10: Backfill*
- Task 11: Framing
- Task 12: Pre-Drywall Walkthrough
- Task 13: Roofing*
- Task 14: Flashings*
- Task 15: Inspections*
- Task 16: Doors and Windows
- Task 17: Plumbing*
- Task 18: Heating*
- Task 19: Electrical*
- Task 20: Inspection
- Task 21: Exterior Finishes
- Task 22: Insulation*
- Task 23: Air-Vapor Barriers*
- Task 24: Cabinet and Electric Review*
- Task 25: Select Interior Finishes
- Task 26: Interior Finishes
- Task 27: Painting*
- Task 28: Cabinets*
- Task 29: Fixtures*
- Task 30: Landscaping*
- Task 31: Pre-Closing Walkthrough
- Task 32: Closing on New Home

Complex Schedule and Cost Model

The first step that the couple did was to develop a complex net-work path model such as the one shown in Figure 8.1. Some required tasks are modeled sequentially, where subsequent tasks cannot be completed unless the previous task is complete. For example, the roof cannot go on unless the structure has been framed, and the excavation work cannot start unless the architectural plans and permits have been approved by the city officials.

Other tasks can be modeled in parallel, such as obtaining bank financing and completing the financial paperwork can be done in parallel with submitting the plans to obtain a permit, or plumbing, heating, and electrical work can be executed concurrently (the plumbers and electricians may be in each other's way but they can still work around each other).

Figures 8.2 and 8.3 illustrate some of the input assumptions the couple and contractor projects each task will cost. The required schedule (in weeks) for each task is also entered. A Monte Carlo risk simulation was run. The results in Figure 8.2 show the critical path of the house building process and Figure 8.3 shows the probability that each path will be the critical path.

Figures 8.4 and 8.5 show the results of the cost and schedule risk profile. While the single-point estimates in Figure 8.3 show $1,230,173 and 38 weeks to complete building their dream home, after running a simulation, the expected or mean cost is actually $1,247,877 and 38.7 weeks. In fact, to be safe, the couple chose a 99th percentile where the cost is sure not to exceed $1,297,404 and 41.4 weeks. This means that they need to have approximately a $50,000 buffer and 3 extra weeks for potential slips in schedule. This might mean the couple will need to hold off getting that new sports car and shift a few weeks to hold that neighborhood block party!

Finally, to reduce the potential schedule slippage, the new homeowners could find ways to mitigate the tasks that are on the critical path. For instance, financing (Task 3) may be taking too long, and they might consider working with a more seasoned mortgage broker rather that doing the paperwork on their own, or that landscaping (Task 30) work can start earlier, once the exterior finishes are done, and so forth. These changes can be made in the model and the computations can be rerun to see the impacts of these modifications.

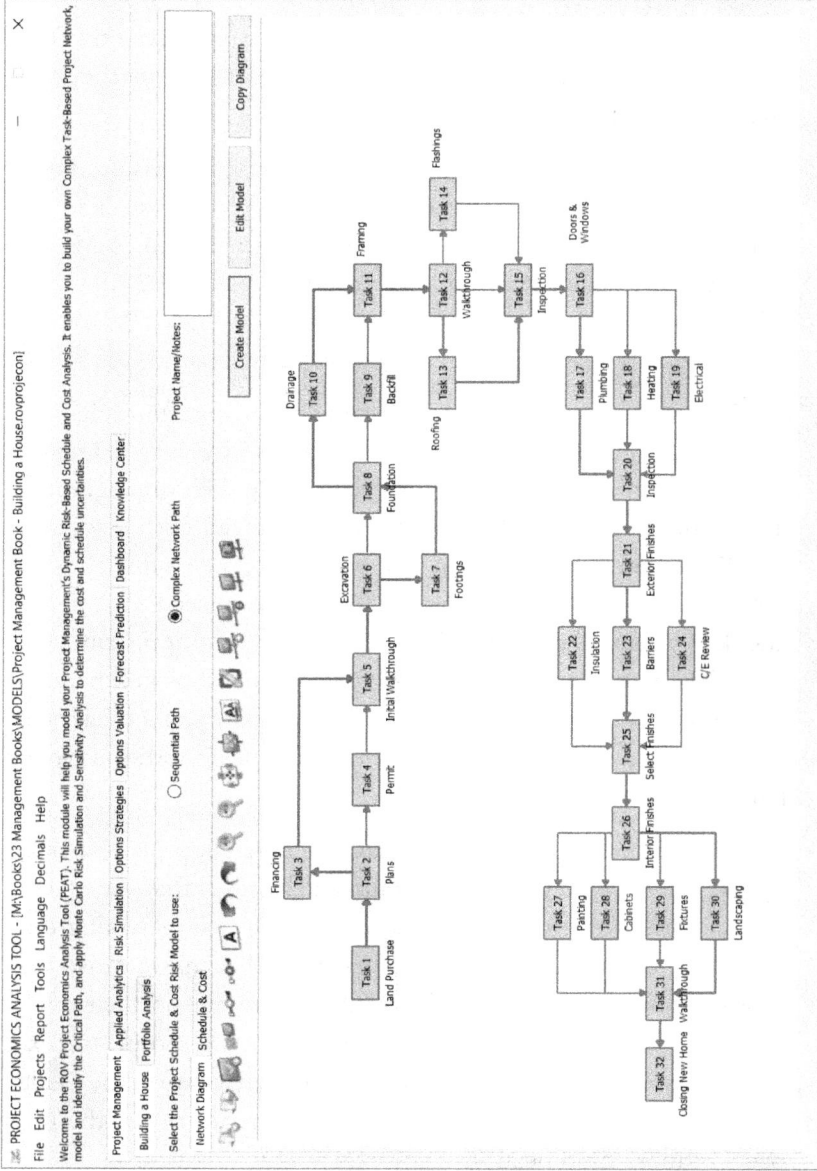

Figure 8.1: Complex Network Path Model

File   Edit   Projects   Report   Tools   Language   Decimals   Help

Welcome to the ROV Project Economics Analysis Tool (PEAT). This module will help you model your Project Management's Dynamic Risk-Based Schedule and Cost Analysis. It enables you to build your own Complex Task-Based Project Network, model and identify the Critical Path, and apply Monte Carlo Risk Simulation and Sensitivity Analysis to determine the cost and schedule uncertainties.

Project Management   Applied Analytics   Risk Simulation   Options Strategies   Options Valuation   Forecast Prediction   Dashboard   Knowledge Center

Building a House   Portfolio Analysis

Select the Project Schedule & Cost Risk Model to use: ○ Sequential Path   ● Complex Network Path   Project Name/Notes:

Network Diagram   Schedule   Schedule & Cost

☑ Include Schedule-Based Cost Analysis   ☑ Perform Risk Simulation
☑ Include Budget Overrun & Buffers   ☑ Apply Seed Value: 123   Simulation Trials: 1,000   Run   Run All Projects
☐ Include Probabilities of Success of Each Task and Model Their Impacts   Show 32   Tasks with   Weekly   ☑ Auto Update   ☐ Run Sequentially

Task	Task Name	Cost (Fixed Cost)			Computed	Time Schedule (Weeks)			Variable	Overrun
		Minimum	Most Lik...	Maximum	Cost	Minimum	Most Lik...	Maximum	Weekly C...	Assump...
Task 1	Land Purchase	800,000	800,000	850,000	800,000	0.5	1	1.5	0	0.00%
Task 2	Plans	5,000	10,000	15,000	13,650	2	3	3	1,000	5.00%
Task 3	Financing	100	100	100	400	2	3	4	100	0.00%
Task 4	Permit	2,000	5,000	6,000	5,000	2	2	4	0	0.00%
Task 5	Initial Walkthrough	100	100	100	200	0.5	1	1.5	100	0.00%
Task 6	Excavation	18,000	20,000	25,000	23,100	1	2	2	1,000	5.00%
Task 7	Footings	5,000	6,000	8,000	7,350	0.5	1	1	1,000	5.00%
Task 8	Foundation	18,000	25,000	35,000	27,300	1	1	1.5	1,000	5.00%
Task 9	Backfill	2,000	4,000	5,000	4,725	0.5	1	1	500	5.00%
Task 10	Drainage	2,000	6,000	8,000	7,088	1	1.5	2	500	5.00%
Task 11	Framing	15,000	28,000	35,000	34,100	3	3	6	1,000	10.00%
Task 12	Walkthrough	100	100	100	200	0.5	1	1.5	100	0.00%
Task 13	Roofing	15,000	20,000	25,000	25,300	2	3	4	1,000	10.00%
Task 14	Flashings	1,000	3,000	3,000	3,675	0.5	1	1.5	500	5.00%
Task 15	Inspection	100	100	100	150	0.5	0.5	0.5	100	0.00%
Task 16	Doors & Windows	10,000	15,000	19,000	17,325	1	1.5	2	1,000	5.00%
Task 17	Plumbing	15,000	18,000	22,000	21,525	2	2.5	3	1,000	5.00%
Task 18	Heating	18,000	25,000	30,000	27,300	1	1	1.5	1,000	5.00%

Triangular

Figure 8.2: Cost and Schedule Assumptions I

PROJECT ECONOMICS ANALYSIS TOOL - [M:\Books\23 Management Books\MODELS\Project Management Book - Building a House.roryprojecon]

File Edit Projects Report Tools Language Decimals Help

Welcome to the ROV Project Economics Analysis Tool (PEAT). This module will help you model your Project Management's Dynamic Risk-Based Schedule and Cost Analysis. It enables you to build your own Complex Task-Based Project Network, model and identify the Critical Path, and apply Monte Carlo Risk Simulation and Sensitivity Analysis to determine the cost and schedule uncertainties.

Project Management | Applied Analytics Risk Simulation Options Valuation Options Strategies Forecast Prediction Dashboard Knowledge Center

Building a House Portfolio Analysis

Select the Project Schedule & Cost Risk Model to use: ○ Sequential Path ● Complex Network Path   Project Name/Notes:

Network Diagram Schedule & Cost

☑ Include Schedule-Based Cost Analysis   ☑ Perform Risk Simulation   Run   Run All Projects
☑ Include Budget Overrun & Buffers   ☑ Apply Seed Value: 1.000   Simulation Trials: 123   ☑ Auto Update   ☐ Run Sequentially
☐ Include Probabilities of Success of Each Task and Model Their Impacts   32

		Show				Weekly			Triangular	
Task 19	Electrical	8.000	12,000	15.000	16,675	2	2.5	3	1,000	15.00%
Task 20	Inspection	100	100	100	150	0.5	0.5	0.5	100	0.00%
Task 21	Exterior Finishes	4,000	5,000	8,000	6,563	2	2.5	3	500	5.00%
Task 22	Insulation	3,000	3,500	4,000	4,200	1	1	2	500	5.00%
Task 23	Barriers	2,000	3,000	5,000	3,938	1	1.5	2	500	5.00%
Task 24	C/E Review	100	100	100	150	0.5	0.5	0.5	100	0.00%
Task 25	Select Finishes	50,000	85,000	115,000	93,610	1	1	1	100	10.00%
Task 26	Interior Finishes	35,000	45,000	65,000	51,450	3	4	5	1,000	5.00%
Task 27	Painting	4,000	5,000	8,000	6,300	2	2	3	500	5.00%
Task 28	Cabinets	2,000	3,000	5,000	4,200	1	2	3	500	5.00%
Task 29	Fixtures	5,000	8,000	12,000	9,450	1	2	3	500	5.00%
Task 30	Landscaping	8,000	10,000	15,000	15,000	2	2.5	3	1,000	20.00%
Task 31	Walkthrough	0	0	0	50	0.5	0.5	0.5	100	0.00%
Task 32	Closing New Home	0	0	0	50	0.5	0.5	0.5	100	0.00%
	Project Total	1,047,600	1,165,100	1,338,600	1,230,173					
	Expected Total Duration					28	38.00	49	65,073	

Critical Path 1-3, 5-8, 10-13, 15-17, 20-21, 23, 25-26, 30-32   13.60%
Critical Path 1-3, 5-8, 10-13, 15-16, 19-21, 23, 25-26, 30-32   13.10%
Critical Path 1-3, 5-8, 10-13, 15-16, 19-22, 25-26, 30-32   6.90%
Critical Path 1-3, 5-8, 10-13, 15-16, 19-21, 23, 25-27, 31-32   6.70%

Figure 8.3: Cost and Schedule Assumptions II

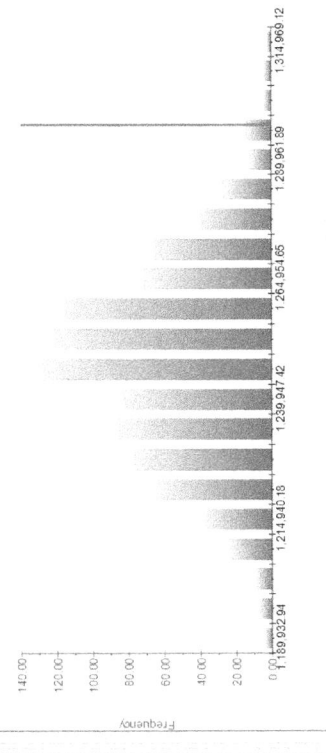

Figure 8.4: Simulated Cost

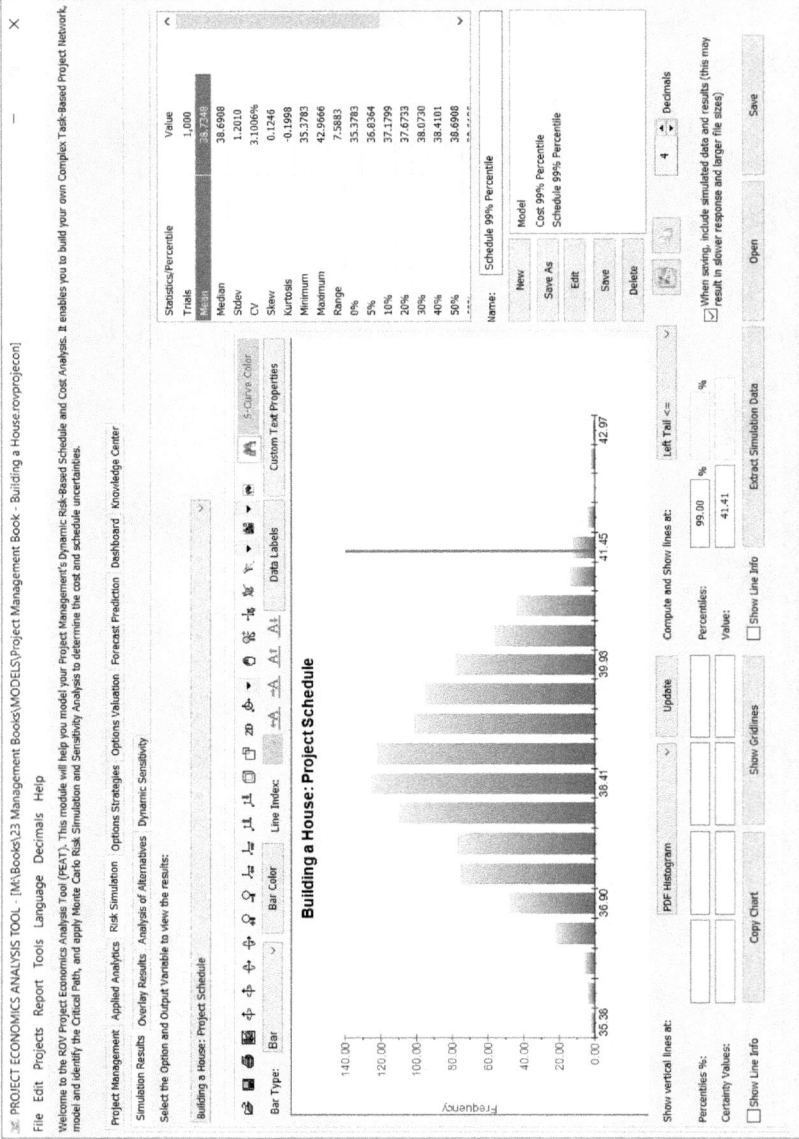

Figure 8.5: Simulated Schedule

APPENDIX A: THE BASICS OF INTERPRETING PDF, CDF, & ICDF CHARTS

This appendix briefly explains the probability density function (PDF) for continuous distributions, which is also called the probability mass function (PMF) for discrete distributions (we use these terms interchangeably), where given some distribution and its parameters, we can determine the probability of occurrence given some outcome or random variable x. In addition, the cumulative distribution function (CDF) can also be computed, which is the sum of the PDF values up to this x value. Finally, the inverse cumulative distribution function (ICDF) is used to compute the value x given the cumulative probability of occurrence.

In mathematics and Monte Carlo risk simulation, a probability density function (PDF) represents a continuous probability distribution in terms of integrals. If a probability distribution has a density of $f(x)$, then, intuitively, the infinitesimal interval of $[x, x + dx]$ has a probability of $f(x)dx$. The PDF, therefore, can be seen as a smoothed version of a probability histogram; that is, by providing an empirically large sample of a continuous random variable repeatedly, the histogram using very narrow ranges will resemble the random variable's PDF. The probability of the interval between $[a, b]$ is given by $\int_a^b f(x)dx$, which means that the total integral of the function f must be 1.0.

It is a common mistake to incorrectly think of $f(a)$ as the probability of a. In fact, $f(a)$ can sometimes be larger than 1 (consider a uniform distribution between 0.0 and 0.5). The random variable x within this distribution will have $f(x)$ greater than 1. The probability, in reality, is the function $f(x)dx$ discussed previously, where dx is an infinitesimal amount.

The cumulative distribution function (CDF) is denoted as $F(x) = P(X \leq x)$, indicating the probability of X taking on a less than or equal value to x. Every CDF is monotonically increasing, is continuous from the right, and at the limits has the following properties: $\lim_{x \to -\infty} F(x) = 0$ and $\lim_{x \to +\infty} F(x) = 1$.

Further, the CDF is related to the PDF by $F(b) - F(a) = P(a \leq X \leq b) = \int_a^b f(x)dx$, where the PDF function f is the derivative of the CDF function F. In probability theory, a probability mass function, or PMF, gives the probability that a discrete random variable is exactly equal to some value. The PMF differs from the PDF in that the values of the latter, defined only for continuous random variables, are not probabilities; rather, its integral over a set of possible values of the random variable is a probability. A random variable is discrete if its probability distribution is discrete and can be characterized by a PMF.

Therefore, X is a discrete random variable if

$$\sum_u P(X = u) = 1$$

as u runs through all possible values of the random variable X.

Interpreting Probability Charts

Here are some tips to help decipher the characteristics of a distribution when looking at different PDF and CDF charts:

- For each distribution, a continuous distribution's PDF is shown as an area chart (Figure A.1) whereas a discrete distribution's PMF is shown as a bar chart (Figure A.2).

- If the distribution can only take a single shape (e.g., normal distributions are always bell shaped, with the only difference being the central tendency measured by the mean and the spread measured by the standard deviation), then typically only one PDF area chart will be shown with an overlay PDF line chart (Figure A.3) showing the effects of various parameters on the distribution.

- The CDF charts, or S-Curves, are shown as line charts (Figure A.4), and sometimes as bar graphs.

- The central tendency of a distribution (e.g., the mean of a normal distribution) is its central location (Figure A.3).

- Multiple area charts and line charts will be shown (e.g., beta distribution) if the distribution can take on multiple shapes (e.g., the beta distribution is a uniform distribution when *alpha* = *beta* = 1; a parabolic distribution when *alpha* = *beta* = 2; a triangular distribution when *alpha* = 1 and *beta* = 2, or vice versa; a positively skewed distribution when *alpha* = 2 and *beta* = 5, and so forth). In this case, you will see multiple area charts and line charts (Figure A.5).

- The starting point of the distribution is sometimes its minimum parameter (e.g., parabolic, triangular, uniform, arcsine, etc.) or its location parameter (e.g., the beta distribution's starting location is 0, but a beta 4 distribution's starting point is the location parameter; Figure A.5 shows a beta 4 distribution with location = 10, its starting point on the x-axis).

- The ending point of the distribution is sometimes its maximum parameter (e.g., parabolic, triangular, uniform, arcsine, etc.) or its natural maximum multiplied by the factor parameter shifted by a location parameter (e.g., the original beta distribution has a minimum of 0 and maximum value of 1, but a beta 4 distribution with location = 10 and factor = 2 indicates that the shifted starting point is 10 and ending point is 11, and its width of 1 is multiplied by a factor of 2, which means that the beta 4 distribution now will have an ending value of 12, as shown in Figure A.5).

- Interactions between parameters are sometimes evident. For example, in the beta 4 distribution, if the alpha = beta, the distribution is symmetrical, whereas it is more positively skewed the greater the difference between beta and alpha, and the more negatively skewed, the greater the difference between alpha and beta (Figure A.6).

- Sometimes a distribution's PDF is shaped by two or three parameters called *shape*, *scale*, and *location*. For instance, the Laplace distribution has two input parameters, alpha location and beta scale, where alpha indicates the central tendency of the distribution (like the mean in a normal distribution) and beta indicates the spread from the mean (like the standard deviation in a normal distribution).

- The narrower the PDF (Figure A.3's normal distribution with a mean of 10 and standard deviation of 2), the steeper the CDF S-Curve looks (Figure A.4), and the smaller the width on the CDF curve.

- A 45-degree straight line CDF (an imaginary straight line connecting the starting and ending points of the CDF) indicates a uniform distribution; an S-Curve CDF with equal amounts above and below the 45-degree straight line indicates a symmetrical and somewhat bell- or mound-shaped curve; a CDF completely curved above the 45-degree line indicates a positively skewed distribution (Figure A.7), while a CDF completely curved below the 45-degree line indicates a negatively skewed distribution (Figure A.8).

- A CDF line that looks identical in shape but shifted to the right or left indicates the same distribution but shifted by some location, and a CDF line that starts from the same point but is pulled both to the left and right indicates a multiplicative effect on the distribution such as a factor multiplication, as shown in Figures A.9 and A.10.

- An almost vertical CDF indicates a high kurtosis distribution with fat tails, and where the center of the distribution is pulled up (e.g., see the Cauchy distribution) versus a relatively flat CDF, a very wide and perhaps flat-tailed distribution is indicated.

- Some discrete distributions can be approximated by a continuous distribution if its number of trials is sufficiently large and its probability of success and failure is fairly symmetrical (e.g., see the binomial and negative binomial distributions). For instance, with a small number of trials and a low probability of success, the binomial distribution is positively skewed, whereas it approaches a symmetrical normal distribution when the number of trials is high, and the probability of success is around 0.50.

- Many distributions are both flexible and interchangeable–refer to the details of each distribution—e.g., binomial is Bernoulli repeated multiple times; arcsine and parabolic are special cases of beta; Pascal is a shifted negative binomial; binomial and Poisson approach normal at the limit; chi-square is the squared sum of multiple normal; Erlang is a special case of gamma; exponential is the inverse of the Poisson but on a continuous basis; F is the ratio of two chi-squares; gamma is related to the lognormal, exponential, Pascal, Erlang, Poisson, and chi-square distributions; Laplace comprises two exponential distributions in one; the log of a lognormal approaches normal; the sum of multiple discrete uniforms approach normal; Pearson V is the inverse of gamma; Pearson VI is the ratio of two gammas; PERT is a modified beta; a large degree of freedom T approaches normal; Rayleigh is a modified Weibull; and so forth.

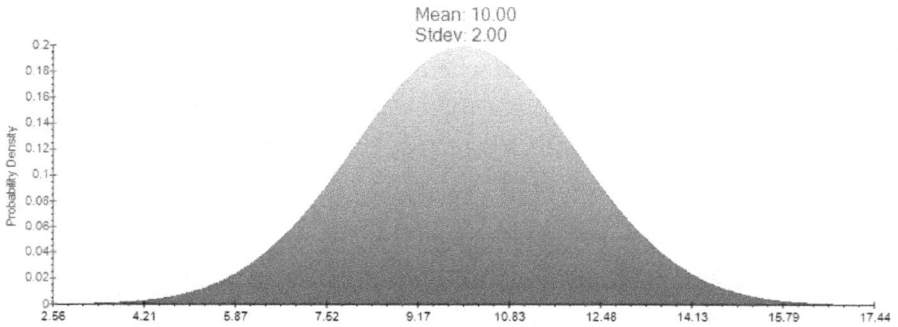

Figure A.1: Continuous PDF (Area Chart)

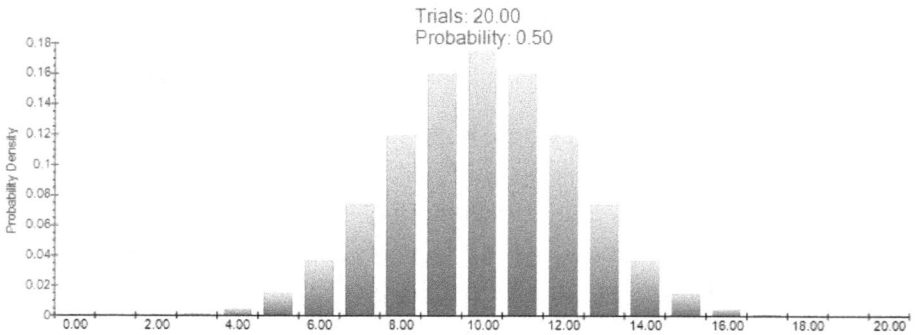

Figure A.2: Discrete PMF (Bar Chart)

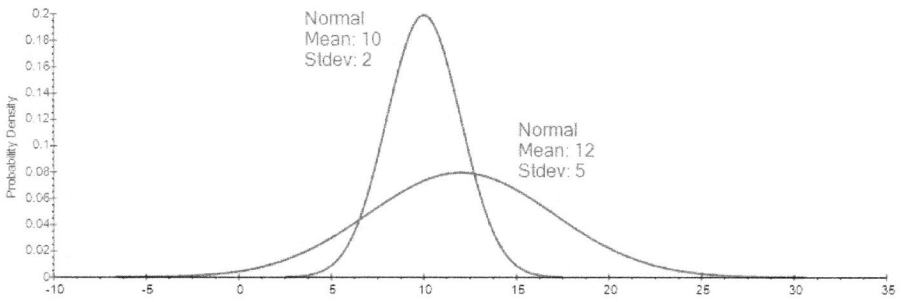

Figure A.3: Multiple Continuous PDF Overlay Charts

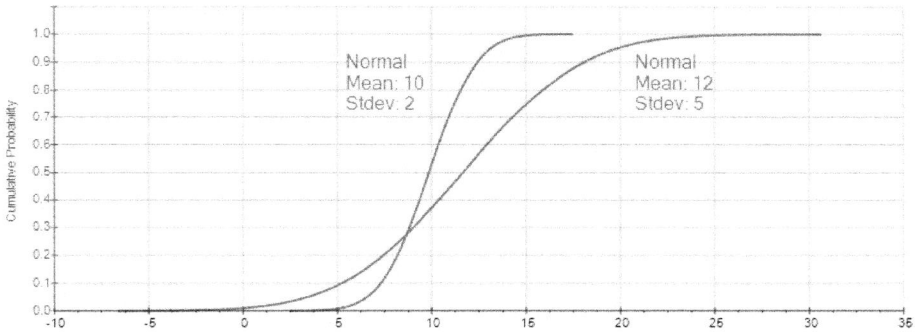

Figure A.4: CDF Overlay Charts

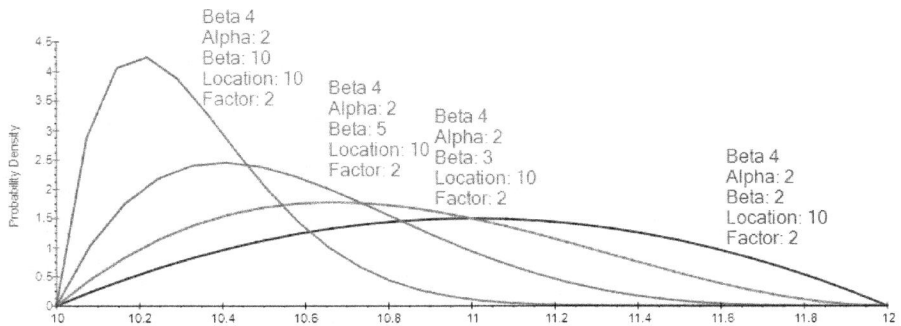

Figure A.5: PDF Characteristics of the Beta Distribution

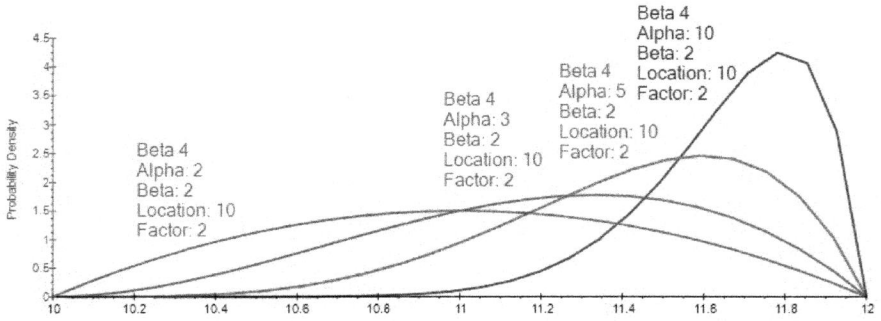

Figure A.6: PDF of a Negatively Skewed Beta Distribution

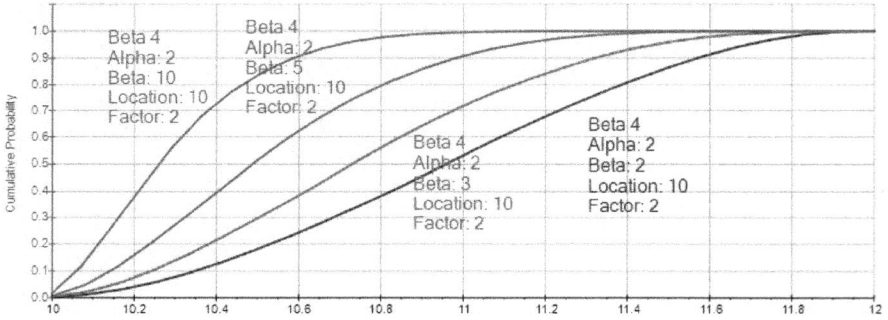

Figure A.7: CDF of a Positively Skewed Distribution

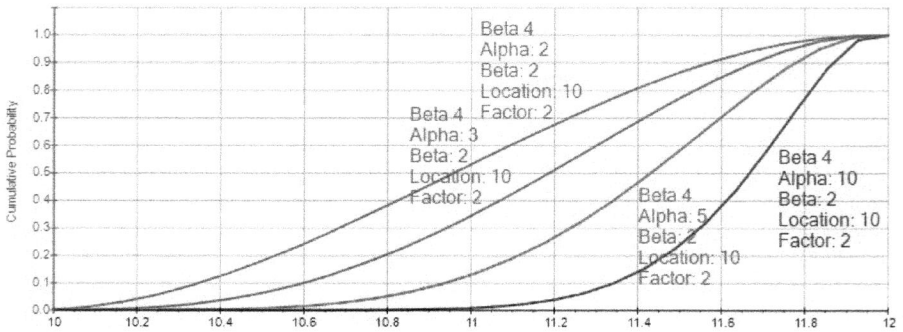

Figure A.8: CDF of a Negatively Skewed Distribution

114

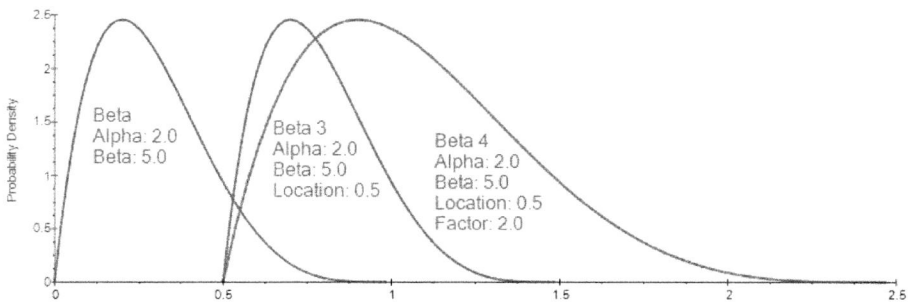

Figure A.9: PDF Characteristics of a Shift

Beta
Alpha: 2.0
Beta: 5.0

Beta 3
Alpha: 2.0
Beta: 5.0
Location: 0.5

Beta 4
Alpha: 2.0
Beta: 5.0
Location: 0.5
Factor: 2.0

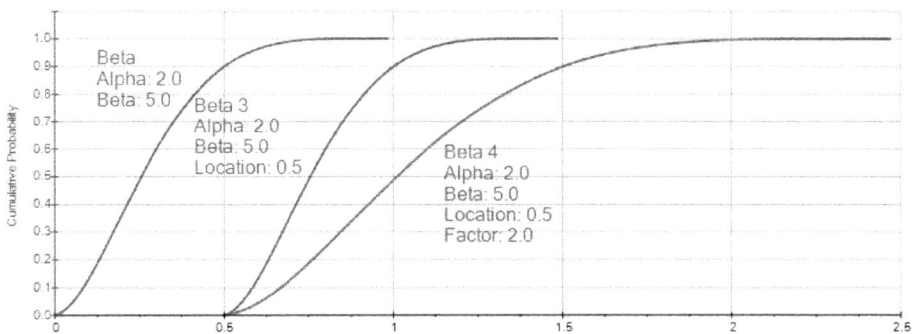

Figure A.10: CDF Characteristics of a Shift

Beta
Alpha: 2.0
Beta: 5.0

Beta 3
Alpha: 2.0
Beta: 5.0
Location: 0.5

Beta 4
Alpha: 2.0
Beta: 5.0
Location: 0.5
Factor: 2.0

APPENDIX B: DISTRIBUTIONAL MOMENTS

The study of statistics refers to the collection, presentation, analysis, and utilization of numerical data to infer and make decisions in the face of uncertainty, where the actual population data is unknown. There are two branches in the study of statistics: descriptive statistics, where data is summarized and described, and inferential statistics, where the population is generalized through a small random sample, making it useful for making predictions or decisions when the population characteristics are unknown.

A *sample* can be defined as a subset of the population being measured; the *population* can be defined as all possible observations of interest of a variable. For instance, if one is interested in the voting practices of all U.S. registered voters, the entire pool of a hundred million registered voters is considered the population while a small survey of one thousand registered voters taken from several small towns across the nation is the sample. The calculated characteristics of the sample (e.g., mean, median, standard deviation) are termed *statistics*, while *parameters* imply that the entire population has been surveyed and the results tabulated. Thus, in decision making, the statistic is of vital importance considering that sometimes the entire population is yet unknown (e.g., who are all your customers, what is the total market share, and so forth) or it is very difficult to obtain all relevant information on the population because it would be too time- or resource-consuming.

In inferential statistics, the following are the usual steps in conducting research:

- Designing the experiment—this phase includes designing the ways to collect all possible and relevant data.

    o Collection of sample data—data is gathered and tabulated.

    o Analysis of data—statistical analysis is performed.

    o Estimation or prediction—inferences are made based on the statistics obtained.

    o Hypothesis testing—decisions are tested against the data to see the outcomes.

- Determining goodness-of-fit—actual data is compared to historical data to see how accurate, valid, and reliable the inference may be.

- Decision making—decisions are made based on the outcome of the inference.

Measuring the Center of the Distribution—The First Moment

The first moments of a distribution of outcomes measure the expected rate of return on a particular project. They measure the location of the project's scenarios and possible outcomes on average. The common statistics for the first moment include the *mean* (average), *median* (center of a distribution), and *mode* (most commonly occurring value). Figure B.1 illustrates the first moment—where in this case, the first moment of this distribution is measured by the mean (μ) or average value.

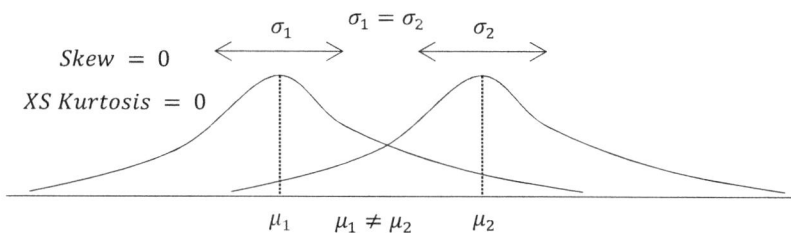

Figure B.1: First Moment

Measuring the Spread of the Distribution—The Second Moment

The second moment measures the spread of a distribution, which is a measure of risk. The spread or width of a distribution indicates the variability of a variable, that is, the potentiality that the variable can fall into different regions of the distribution—in other words, the potential scenarios of outcomes. Figure B.2 illustrates two distributions with identical first moments (identical means) but very different second moments or risks. The visualization becomes clearer in Figure B.3. As an example, suppose there are two stocks and the first stock's movements (the solid line) with the smaller fluctuation is compared against the second stock's movements (the dotted line) with a much higher price fluctuation. Clearly an investor would view the stock with the wilder fluctuation as riskier because the outcomes of the riskier stock are relatively more unknown than the less risky stock. The vertical axis in Figure B.3 measures the stock prices; thus, the riskier stock has a wider range of potential outcomes. This range is translated into a distribution's width (the horizontal axis) in Figure B.2, where the wider distribution represents the riskier asset. Hence, width or spread of a distribution measures a variable's risks. Notice that in Figure B.2, both distributions have identical first moments or central tendencies but clearly the distributions are very different. This difference in the distributional width is measurable. Mathematically and statistically, the width or risk of a variable can be measured through several different statistics, including the range, standard deviation (σ), variance, coefficient of variation, and percentiles.

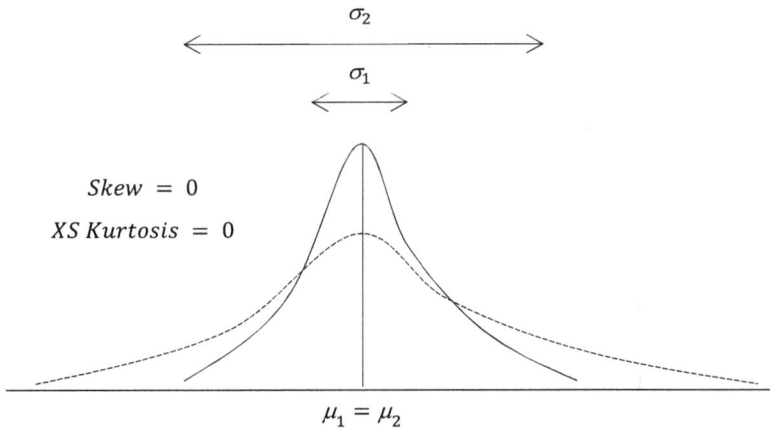

$$\sigma_2$$

$$\sigma_1$$

$Skew = 0$

$XS\ Kurtosis = 0$

$$\mu_1 = \mu_2$$

Figure B.2: Second Moment

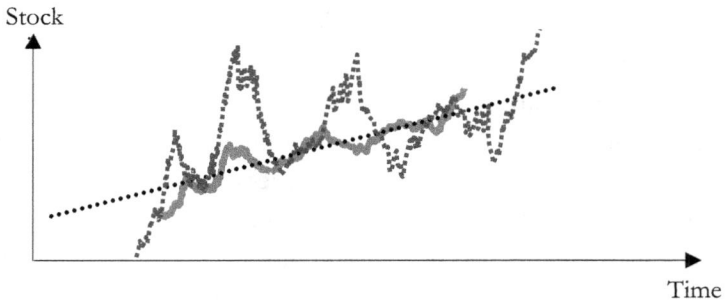

Stock

Time

Figure B.3: Stock Price Fluctuations

Variance and Standard Deviation

Variance and standard deviation are two common measures of the second moment. Variance is the average of the squared deviations about their means, in squared units:

$$\sigma^2 = \sum_{i=1}^{N} \frac{(x_i - \mu)^2}{N} \text{ and } s^2 = \sum_{i=1}^{n} \frac{(x_i - \bar{x})^2}{n - 1}$$

Standard deviation is in original units and, thus, useful as a direct means of comparison of dispersion and variability measured in the same units:

$$\sigma = \sqrt{\sum_{i=1}^{N} \frac{(x_i - \mu)^2}{N}} \text{ and } s = \sqrt{\sum_{i=1}^{n} \frac{(x_i - \bar{x})^2}{n - 1}}$$

Although standard deviation and variances have many uses, those uses are limited because their measurements are in the same units and, hence, are considered absolute values of risk.

Coefficient of Variation

The coefficient of variation (CV) is unitless and measures relative variability. It thus allows the comparison of two datasets to see which has more variability without worrying about the units. In comparison, standard deviations are absolute measures of variability and depend heavily on the data's unit of measure.

$$CV = \frac{s}{\bar{x}} \text{ or } CV = \frac{\sigma}{\mu}$$

EXAMPLE

Statistic	# in family	Food expenditure ($)
$\bar{x}$	3.23	$110.5
s	1.34	$25.25

Which has more variation, the number of family members or the food expenditure?

CV in family $= 1.34/3.23 = 0.415$

CV in expenditures $= 25.25/110.25 = 0.229$

The calculations show that there is more variation in the number of family members.

Measuring the Skew of the Distribution—The Third Moment

The third moment measures a distribution's skewness, that is, how the distribution is pulled to one side or the other. Figure B.4 illustrates a negative or left skew (the tail of the distribution points to the left) and Figure B.5 illustrates a positive or right skew (the tail of the distribution points to the right). The mean is always skewed towards the tail of the distribution, while the median remains constant. Another way of seeing this is that the mean moves but the standard deviation, variance, or width may still remain constant. If the third moment is not considered, then looking only at the expected returns (mean) and risk (standard deviation), a positively skewed project might be incorrectly chosen! For example, if the horizontal axis represents the net revenues of a project, then clearly a left or negatively skewed distribution might be preferred as there is a higher probability of greater returns (Figure B.4) as compared to a higher probability for a lower level of returns (Figure B.5). Thus, in a skewed distribution, the median is a better measure of returns, as the medians for both Figures B.4 and B.5 are identical, risks are identical, and, hence, a project with a negatively skewed distribution of net profits is a better choice. Failure to account for a project's distributional skewness may mean that the incorrect project may be chosen (e.g., two projects may have identical first and second moments, that is, they both have identical returns and risk profiles, but their distributional skews may be very different). Skew is calculated by:

$$Skew = \frac{n}{(n-1)(n-2)} \sum_{i=1}^{n} \left(\frac{x_i - \bar{x}}{s}\right)^3$$

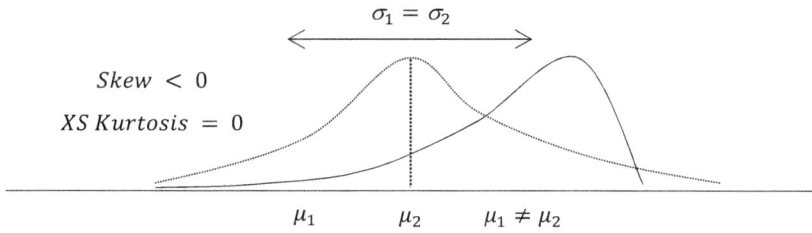

Figure B.4: Third Moment (Left Skew)

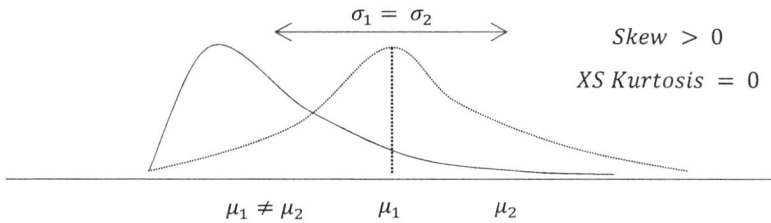

Figure B.5: Third Moment (Right Skew)

Measuring the Catastrophic Tail Events in a Distribution— The Fourth Moment

The fourth moment, or kurtosis, measures the peakedness of a distribution. Figure B.6 illustrates this effect. The background is a normal distribution with a kurtosis of 3.0 or an excess kurtosis of 0 (XS kurtosis is defined as the kurtosis difference from a normal distribution). The new distribution has a higher kurtosis, thus the area under the curve is thicker at the tails with less area in the central body. This condition has major impacts on uncertainty analysis because for the two distributions in Figure B.6, the first three moments (mean, standard deviation, and skewness) can be identical but the fourth moment (kurtosis) is different. This means that although the expected returns and uncertainties are identical, the probabilities of extreme and catastrophic events (potential large losses or large gains) occurring are higher for a high kurtosis distribution (e.g., stock market returns are leptokurtic or have high kurtosis). Ignoring a project's return's kurtosis may be detrimental. Kurtosis is defined as:

$$Kurtosis = \frac{n(n+1)}{(n-1)(n-2)(n-3)} \sum_{i=1}^{n} \left(\frac{x_i - \bar{x}}{s}\right)^4 - \frac{3(n-1)^2}{(n-2)(n-3)}$$

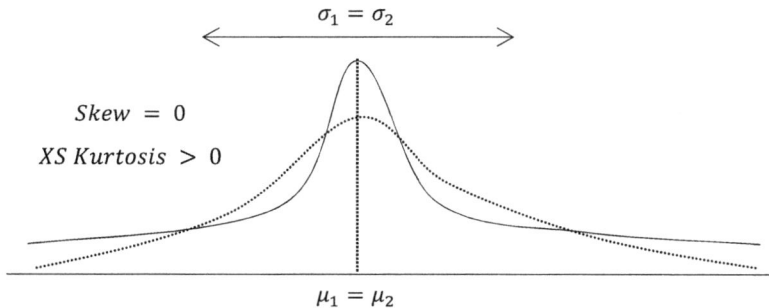

$$\sigma_1 = \sigma_2$$

$Skew = 0$

$XS\ Kurtosis > 0$

$$\mu_1 = \mu_2$$

Figure B.6: Fourth Moment

Most distributions can be defined by up to four moments. The first moment describes a distribution's location or central tendency (expected value); the second moment describes its width or spread (uncertainty); the third moment, its directional skew (most probable events); and the fourth moment, its peakedness or thickness in the tails (catastrophic extreme tail events). All four moments should be calculated and interpreted to provide a more comprehensive view of the project under analysis.

APPENDIX C:
MONTE CARLO
RISK SIMULATION

Monte Carlo simulation, named for the famous gambling capital of Monaco, is a very potent methodology. For the practitioner, simulation opens the door for solving difficult and complex but practical problems with great ease. Perhaps the most famous early use of Monte Carlo simulation was by the Nobel physicist Enrico Fermi (sometimes referred to as the father of the atomic bomb) in 1930, when he used a random method to calculate the properties of the newly discovered neutron. Monte Carlo methods were central to the simulations required for the Manhattan Project, where in the 1950s Monte Carlo simulation was used at Los Alamos for early work relating to the development of the hydrogen bomb and became popularized in the fields of physics and operations research. The RAND Corporation and the U.S. Air Force were two of the major organizations responsible for funding and disseminating information on Monte Carlo methods during this time, and today there is a wide application of Monte Carlo simulation in many different fields including engineering, physics, research and development, business, and finance.

Simplistically, Monte Carlo simulation creates artificial futures by generating thousands and even hundreds of thousands of sample paths of outcomes and analyzes their prevalent characteristics. In practice, Monte Carlo simulation methods are used for risk analysis, risk quantification, sensitivity analysis, and prediction. An alternative to simulation is the use of highly complex stochastic closed-form mathematical models. For analysts in a company, taking graduate-level advanced math and statistics courses is just not logical or practical. A brilliant analyst would use all available tools at his or her disposal to obtain the same answer the easiest and most practical way possible. And in all cases, when modeled correctly, Monte Carlo simulation provides similar answers to the more mathematically elegant methods. In addition, there are many real-life applications where closed-form models do not exist and the only recourse is to apply simulation methods. So, what exactly is Monte Carlo simulation and how does it work?

What Is Simulation?

Today, high-speed computers have made possible many complex computations that were seemingly intractable in the past. For scientists, engineers, statisticians, managers, business analysts, and others, computers have made it possible to create models that simulate reality and aid in making predictions. One such model is used in simulating real systems by accounting for randomness and future uncertainties through investigating hundreds and even thousands of different scenarios. The results are then compiled and used to make decisions. This is what Monte Carlo simulation is all about.

Monte Carlo simulation in its simplest form is a random number generator that is useful for forecasting, estimation, and risk analysis. A simulation calculates numerous scenarios of a model by repeatedly picking values from a user-predefined *probability distribution* for the uncertain variables and using those values for the model. As all those scenarios produce associated results in a model, each scenario can have a forecast. Forecasts are events (usually with formulas or functions) that you define as important outputs of the model.

Think of the Monte Carlo simulation approach as picking golf balls out of a large basket repeatedly with replacement. The size and shape of the basket depend on the distributional *Input Assumption* (e.g., a normal distribution with a mean of 100 and a standard deviation of 10, versus a uniform distribution or a triangular distribution) where some baskets are deeper or more symmetrical than others, allowing certain balls to be pulled out more frequently than others. The number of balls pulled repeatedly depends on the number of *Trials* simulated. For a large model with multiple related assumptions, imagine the large model as a very large basket, where many baby baskets reside. Each baby basket has its own set of colored golf balls that are bouncing around. Sometimes these baby baskets are linked with each other (if there is a *Correlation* between the variables), forcing the golf balls to bounce in tandem whereas in other uncorrelated cases, the balls are bouncing independently of one another. The balls that are picked each time from these interactions within the model (the large basket) are tabulated and recorded, providing a *Forecast Output* result of the simulation.

Understanding Probability Distributions

This appendix demonstrates the power of Monte Carlo risk simulation but in order to get started with simulation, one first needs to understand the concept of probability distributions. This appendix continues with the use of the author's *Risk Simulator* software and shows how simulation can be very easily and effortlessly implemented in an existing Excel model. A limited trial version of the *Risk Simulator* software (to obtain a permanent version, please visit *www.realoptionsvaluation.com*). Professors can obtain free semester-long computer lab licenses for their students and themselves if this book and the simulation/options valuation software are used and taught in an entire class.

To begin to understand probability, consider this example: You want to look at the distribution of nonexempt wages within one department of a large company. First, you gather raw data—in this case, the wages of each nonexempt employee in the department. Second, you organize the data into a meaningful format and plot the data as a frequency distribution on a chart. To create a frequency distribution, you divide the wages into group intervals and list these intervals on the chart's horizontal axis. Then you list the number or frequency of employees in each interval on the chart's vertical axis. Now you can easily see the distribution of nonexempt wages within the department.

A glance at the chart illustrated in Figure C.1 reveals that the employees earn from $7.00 to $9.00 per hour. You can chart this data as a probability distribution. A probability distribution shows the number of employees in each interval as a fraction of the total number of employees. To create a probability distribution, you divide the number of employees in each interval by the total number of employees and list the results on the chart's vertical axis.

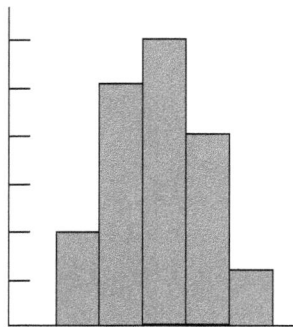

Figure C.1: Frequency Histogram I

The chart in Figure C.2 shows the number of employees in each wage group as a fraction of all employees; you can estimate the likelihood or probability that an employee drawn at random from the whole group earns a wage within a given interval. For example, assuming the same conditions exist at the time the sample was taken, the probability is 0.20 (a one in five chance) that an employee drawn at random from the whole group earns $8.50 an hour.

Probability distributions are either discrete or continuous. *Discrete probability distributions* describe distinct values, usually integers, with no intermediate values and are shown as a series of vertical bars. A discrete distribution, for example, might describe the number of heads in four flips of a coin as 0, 1, 2, 3, or 4. *Continuous probability distributions* are actually mathematical abstractions because they assume the existence of every possible intermediate value between two numbers; that is, a continuous distribution assumes there is an infinite number of values between any two points in the distribution. However, in many situations, you can effectively use a continuous distribution to approximate a discrete distribution even though the continuous model does not necessarily describe the situation exactly.

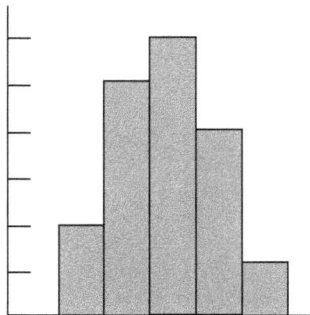

Figure C.2: Frequency Histogram II

Selecting a Probability Distribution

Plotting data is one method for selecting a probability distribution. The following steps provide another process for selecting probability distributions that best describe the uncertain variables in your spreadsheets. To select the correct probability distribution, use the following steps:

- Look at the variable in question. List everything you know about the conditions surrounding this variable. You might be able to gather valuable information about the uncertain variable from historical data. If historical data are not available, use your own judgment, based on experience, listing everything you know about the uncertain variable.

- Review the descriptions of the probability distributions.

- Select the distribution that characterizes this variable. A distribution characterizes a variable when the conditions of the distribution match those of the variable.

Alternatively, if you have historical, comparable, contemporaneous, or forecast data, you can use Risk Simulator's distributional fitting modules to find the best statistical fit for your existing data. This fitting process will apply some advanced statistical techniques to find the best distribution and its relevant parameters that describe the data.

There are over 50 probability distributions available in Risk Simulator but only a few are commonly used in project management. Following is a detailed listing of only the most commonly used types of continuous probability distributions that can be used in Monte Carlo simulation.

Lognormal Distribution

The lognormal distribution is widely used in situations where values are positively skewed, for example, in financial analysis for security valuation or in real estate for property valuation, and where values cannot fall below zero.

Stock prices are usually positively skewed rather than normally (symmetrically) distributed. Stock prices exhibit this trend because they cannot fall below the lower limit of zero but might increase to any price without limit. Similarly, real estate prices illustrate positive skewness and are lognormally distributed as property values cannot become negative.

The conditions underlying the lognormal distribution are:

The uncertain variable can increase without limits but cannot fall below zero.

The uncertain variable is positively skewed, with most of the values near the lower limit.

The natural logarithm of the uncertain variable yields a normal distribution.

Generally, if the coefficient of variability is greater than 30%, use a lognormal distribution. Otherwise, use the normal distribution.

The mathematical constructs for the lognormal distribution are as follows:

$$f(x) = \frac{1}{x\sqrt{2\pi}\,ln(\sigma)}\,e^{\frac{-[ln(x)-ln(\mu)]^2}{2[ln(\sigma)]^2}} \quad for\ x > 0;\ \mu > 0\ and\ \sigma > 0$$

$$Mean\ =\ exp\left(\mu + \frac{\sigma^2}{2}\right)$$

$$Standard\ Deviation\ =\ \sqrt{exp(\sigma^2 + 2\mu)\,[exp(\sigma^2) - 1]}$$

$$Skewness\ =\ \left[\sqrt{exp(\sigma^2) - 1}\right](2 + exp(\sigma^2))$$

$$Excess\ Kurtosis\ =\ exp\ (4\sigma^2) + 2\,exp\ (3\sigma^2) + 3\,exp\ (2\sigma^2) - 6$$

Mean (μ) and standard deviation (σ) are the distributional parameters.

Input requirements: Mean and standard deviation both > 0 and can be any positive value.

Lognormal Parameter Sets: By default, the lognormal distribution uses the arithmetic mean and standard deviation. For applications for which historical data are available, it is more appropriate to use either the logarithmic mean and standard deviation, or the geometric mean and standard deviation.

Lognormal 3 Distribution

The lognormal 3 distribution uses the same constructs as the original lognormal distribution but adds a location, or shift, parameter. The lognormal distribution starts from a minimum value of 0, whereas this lognormal 3, or shifted lognormal, distribution shifts the starting location to any other value.

Mean, standard deviation, and location (shift) are the distributional parameters. Input requirements:

$Mean > 0\ and\ Standard\ Deviation > 0$

Location can be any positive or negative value including zero.

Normal Distribution

The normal distribution is the most important distribution in probability theory because it describes many natural phenomena, such as people's IQs or heights. Decision makers can use the normal distribution to describe uncertain variables such as the inflation rate or the future price of gasoline.

The three conditions underlying the normal distribution are:

- Some value of the uncertain variable is the most likely (the mean of the distribution).

- The uncertain variable could as likely be above the mean as it could be below the mean (symmetrical about the mean).

- The uncertain variable is more likely in the vicinity of the mean than further away.

The mathematical constructs for the normal distribution are as follows:

$$f(x) = \frac{1}{\sqrt{2\pi}\sigma} e^{\frac{-(x-\mu)^2}{2\sigma^2}} \quad \text{for all values of } x \text{ and } \mu; \text{ while } \sigma > 0$$

$Mean = \mu$

$Standard\ Deviation = \sigma$

$Skewness = 0$ (for all mean and standard deviation)

$Excess\ Kurtosis = 0$ (for all mean and standard deviation)

Mean (μ) and standard deviation (σ) are the distributional parameters. Input requirements: *Standard deviation* > 0 and can be any positive value whereas mean can be any value.

PERT Distribution

The PERT distribution is widely used in project and program management to define the worst-case, nominal-case, and best-case scenarios of project completion time. It is related to the beta and triangular distributions. PERT distribution can be used to identify risks in project and cost models based on the likelihood of meeting targets and goals across any number of project components using minimum, most likely, and maximum values, but it is designed to generate a distribution that more closely resembles realistic probability distributions. The PERT distribution can provide a close fit to the normal or lognormal distributions. Like the triangular distribution, the PERT distribution emphasizes the *most likely* value over the minimum and maximum estimates. However, unlike the triangular distribution, the PERT distribution constructs a smooth curve that places progressively more emphasis on values around (near) the most likely value, in favor of values around the edges. In practice, this means that we *trust* the estimate for the most likely value, and we believe that even if it is not exactly accurate (as estimates seldom are), we have an expectation that the resulting value will be close to that estimate. Assuming that many real-world phenomena are normally distributed, the appeal of the PERT distribution is that it produces a curve similar to the normal curve in shape, without knowing the precise parameters of the related normal curve. Minimum, most likely, and maximum are the distributional parameters.

The mathematical constructs for the PERT distribution are shown below:

$$f(x) = \frac{(x - Min)^{A1-1}(Max - x)^{A2-1}}{B(A1, A2)(Max - Min)^{A1+A2-1}}$$

$$where \ A1 = 6\left[\frac{\dfrac{Min + 4(Likely) + Max}{6} - Min}{Max - Min}\right] \ and \ A2$$

$$= 6\left[\frac{Max - \dfrac{Min + 4(Likely) + Max}{6}}{Max - Min}\right]$$

and B is the Beta function

$$Mean = \frac{Min + 4Mode + Max}{6}$$

$$Standard\ Deviation\ =\ \sqrt{\frac{(\mu-Min)(Max-\mu)}{7}}$$

$$Skew\ =\ \sqrt{\frac{7}{(\mu-Min)(Max-\mu)}}\left(\frac{Min+Max-2\mu}{4}\right)$$

Excess Kurtosis is a complex function and cannot be readily computed. Input requirements: $Min \leq Most\ Likely \leq Max$ and can be positive, negative, or zero.

SOFTWARE DOWNLOAD & INSTALL

As current versions of the software are continually updated, we highly recommend that you visit the Real Options Valuation, Inc., website and follow the instructions below to install the latest software applications.

- **Step 1**: Visit **www.realoptionsvaluation.com** and click on **Downloads** and **Download Software** (Figure A). You will be prompted to log in. Please first register if you are a first-time user (Figure B) and an automated e-mail will be sent to you within several minutes. (If you do not receive a registration e-mail after you register, then please send a note to support@realoptionsvaluation.com.) While waiting for the automated e-mail, browse this page and see the free getting started videos, case studies, and sample models you can download.

- **Step 2**: Return to this site and LOGIN using the login credentials you received via e-mail. Download and install the latest versions of **Risk Simulator** on this Web page. The download links, installation instructions, and Hardware ID information are also presented on this page (Figure C).

- **Step 3**: After installing the software, start Excel and you will see a Risk Simulator ribbon. Follow the instructions provided on the Web page to obtain your Hardware ID and e-mail it to support@realoptionsvaluation.com. Mention the code "**MR3E 30 Days**" and you will be sent a free extended 30-day license to use Risk Simulator. In addition, please indicate in your e-mail that you need the latest version of PEAT and we will send you a link with a 30-day trial license.

Figure A: Step 1 – Software Download Site

Browser tabs/URL bar: Getting Started and Mo × | www.realoptionsvaluation.com/getting-started-and-modelling-videos/

Testimonials | FAQ | Global Partners | Contact Us

Real Options Valuation

🔵 English 🔴 Chinese (Simplified) 🔴 Chinese (Traditional) 🔵 French ⬛ German 🟩 Italian
🔵 Japanese 🔵 Korean 🟦 Portuguese (Brazil) 🔴 Russian 🟨 Spanish

0 items $0.00

CQRM CERTIFICATE | TRAINING | CONSULTING | SOFTWARE | BOOKS | DOWNLOADS | PURCHASE |

SOFTWARE DOWNLOADS

GETTING STARTED AND
MODELLING VIDEOS

PRODUCT BROCHURES

SAMPLE MODELS

WHITEPAPERS AND CASE STUDIES

DOWNLOAD CENTER

You can also visit our mirror download site if you have problems downloading from this page.

Welcome to Real Options Valuation, Inc.'s download center. Here you will be able to download versions of the software you have purchased (license information required to install these full versions), product brochures, case ple training videos to help you get started in using our software, as well as sample Excel models to use with Risk Simulator and Re...   ...ftware.

GETTING STARTED AND MODELING VIDEOS

The following are some live-motion and voice narrated videos which are playable on your computer using Windows Media Player or other video players capable of WMV playback. You can simply click on any of these links below to view the streaming videos.

ROV SOFTWARE GETTING STARTED VIDEOS

We also have some more detailed Risk Analysis and Risk Simulator software getting started videos that you can download and watch. These videos total about 2 hours. For even more detailed training, please check out our set of 12 Training DVDs (over 30 hours) or our hands-on Certified in Risk Management seminars (4 days). The following are updated detailed getting started videos on Risk Simulator, featuring all the new tools such as Auto ARIMA, GARCH, JS Curves, Cubic Spline, Maximum Likelihood, Data Diagnostics, Statistical Analysis, Modeling Toolkit, and more...

Figure A: Step 1 – Software Download Site

DOWNLOAD CENTER

You can also visit our mirror download site if you have problems downloading from this page

Welcome to Real Options Valuation, Inc.'s download center. Here you will be able to download trial versions of our software, full versions of the software you have purchased (license information required to install these full versions), product brochures, case studies and white papers, and sample training videos to help you get started in using our software, as well as sample Excel models to use with Risk Simulator and Real Options Super Lattice Solver software.

YOU ARE REQUIRED TO LOGIN TO VIEW THIS PAGE.

Username

Password

| LOG IN | REGISTER |

Figure B: First-Time Visitor Registration

Real Options Valuation

🌐 English 🀄 Chinese (Simplified) 🀄 Chinese (Traditional) 🇫🇷 French 🇩🇪 German 🇮🇹 Italian
🇯🇵 Japanese 🇰🇷 Korean 🇧🇷 Portuguese (Brazil) 🇷🇺 Russian 🇪🇸 Spanish

CORM CERTIFICATE | TRAINING | CONSULTING | SOFTWARE | BOOKS | DOWNLOADS | PURCHASE

Items \$0.00

FULL & TRIAL VERSION DOWNLOAD:

Download Risk Simulator 2018 – Auto Installer

Download Risk Simulator 2018 – Auto Installer (mirror site)

Download Risk Simulator 2018 – For 32 Bit Excel

Download Risk Simulator 2018 – For 32 Bit Excel (mirror site)

Download Risk Simulator 2018 – For 64 Bit Excel

Download Risk Simulator 2018 – For 64 Bit Excel (mirror site)

Download OLDER version of Risk Simulator 2014 [WIN x64 and Excel x32 edition]

Download OLDER version of Risk Simulator 2014 [WIN x64 and Excel x32 edition] (mirror site)

This is a full version of the software but will expire in 15 days, during which time you can purchase a license to permanently unlock the software. Please first uninstall all previous versions of Risk Simulator before installing this newer version.

To permanently unlock the software, purchase a license and e-mail us your Hardware ID (after installing the software, start Excel, click on Risk Simulator 12-step and e-mail admin@realoptionsvaluation.com the 16 to 20 digit Hardware ID located on the bottom left of the splash screen). We will then e-mail you a permanent license file. Save this file to your hard drive, start Excel, click on Risk Simulator, License Install License and point to the location of this license file, restart Excel and you are now permanently licensed. Installing the license only takes a few seconds.

SYSTEM REQUIREMENTS, FAQ, AND ADDITIONAL RESOURCES:

- Windows 7, 8, and 10 (32 and 64 bits)
- Microsoft Excel 2010, 2013 or 2016
- 2GB RAM Minimum (4 GB recommended)
- 600 MB Hard Drive
- Administrative Rights to install software
- Microsoft .NET Framework 2.0, 3.0, 3.5 or later
- MAC OS users will require either Virtual Machine or Parallels running Microsoft Excel

Figure C: Download Links and Hardware ID Instructions

INDEX

www.ingramcontent.com/pod-product-compliance
Lightning Source LLC
Chambersburg PA
CBHW060041210326
41520CB00009B/1225